In the Heart of MEXICO

Mae Royer
phil . 1:21

MAE R. ROYER

Dedication

This book is dedicated to my fine friends of Mexico who have been so understanding, kind and helpful to me, the overworked doctors, generous Christian businessmen, and self-sacrificing pastors and teachers. These educated and understanding individuals are striving for the uplifting of their people and often receive misunderstanding, criticism and persecution from the fanatical and ignorant. But they continue to go on, bravely struggling against the strong elements opposing progress.

Nor would I forget to mention the dear, sincere humble people, who although underprivileged, are so appreciative and comprehensive. In accepting and allying themselves with new progressive ideals and causes, they often have to suffer beyond measure. They also attribute much to the coming generations of their country and to the Kingdom of God.

Preface

The name of this book was given to me by a fine-looking, Spanish-type university student in Mexico City. He had said, "Señorita, I envy you — your life and work among our Indians in the rural mountain areas. You have an opportunity to know them in a way we Mexicans never can. They are "The Heart of Mexico," but they will never trust nor open up to us. You can share in their sufferings, strivings and hopes, and perhaps even be able to understand them. Some day you must write a book of your experiences in the Indian villages, in the heart of our country."

During the years, as I contemplated writing my story, this book was always visualized as "In the Heart of Mexico."

Keeping a diary during those exciting years of the early 40's made it possible to recall some of these things after so long a time. Other happenings did not need notes, for they are very vivid in my memory. Also, the printed letters and others which I had sent to my friends during that time helped to put the contents in chronological order.

Although all the characters are real and contents true, a few names have been changed, because some of the characters may be sensitive about having their real names used.

Perhaps after reading this story of life as it really is, you will understand why "people who get into the heart of Mexico can never get Mexico out of their hearts."

Introduction

In the Heart of Mexico is the title for this inspiring little volume, but it could well have been called "Inside the Heart of a Young Missionary Nurse." Revealed in these pages, factually but humbly, is the very moving account of one whose heart was gripped first by the love of God, and then by the challenge of missionary medicine.

She vividly describes both the beauty of Aztec country in central Mexico, and the heartache of a people bound by tribal customs.

Because she makes people real to you, Don Julio, and others, will become more than names. You will be both saddened and amused, then again, thrilled as you read. You will long remember Marcos, who might have had a closer relationship with this nurse from the "outside" were it not for wide cultural and religious barriers.

How grateful we should be that the Señorita Royer has taken the time from her busy schedule at El Retiro, her Children's Home and Youth Camp, to record this very personal story. Her contribution, medically, socially and spiritually relates, by this account, to many cultures around the world. With much profit this enlightening material could become required reading for future missionary candidates.

You will come to the close of this book, not just more familiar with the conditions that grip the people in the heart of Mexico; but with a deeper burden to make known the healing liberating message of Christ. Over 50 years ago this same gospel claimed the heart and life of this gifted servant of His, and Mexico has been enriched.

In the Heart of Mexico joins her other two shorter books — *Jewels of Mexico* and *More Jewels of Mexico*, which relate to her mission endeavor during the years. I commend this most recent book to you.

Rev. Duane M. Ray
Director of Missions of the
Evangelical Congregational Church

The setting for this book:
Church and house with clinic in Chapulhuacanito.

CHAPTER

1

The wooden ferry swayed with the current of the winding Moctezuma River, flowing between the lush tropical mountains of the Haustecan (whas-ta-ken) range, where even the rivers are green.

Looking back towards the town of Tamazunchale (the tourists often say, Thomas and Charlie), the figures of friends waving "goodbye" were disappearing in the distance.

"Come back for supplies, when you can, and send us word if you need anything," the Doctora and Rev. Dale had said. It was under their mission that I was going out to the regions beyond to do medical and evangelistic work among the Indians.

Today, the river seemed to be a dividing line between the known and the unknown, the comforts and the primitive, the securities and the uncertainties.

As I leaned over the rail, watching the deep, dark swiftly moving water, disturbing thoughts came rushing through my mind about the new strange life which lay before me. Would I be able to take the hardships and the trials I knew awaited me in the Indian villages out in those mysterious hills? However, life had never been easy, and He who led had never failed. So, deeper than the fears was the assurance that the God of the past was also the God of the future. When Christ had so vividly called me to follow Him, I knew it was to be to the uttermost. Fortunately, there is the natural appeal of romance in the unusual and the adventure of the unknown to help beckon us on.

"Whoa, whoa there, whoa," shouted the mule drivers, as the ferry reached the other side and the animals became restless.

"Better mount your burro before you get crushed in the rush to get off," advised Don Miguel, my guide, a fine looking, well-built Mexican man, who was a native evangelist with the Dales. Jose, our Indian brother, was already pushing to the front with his donkey, carrying the medicines and a few other supplies.

There were no roads in this section at the time, in the early forties, only the well-beaten mule path, which curved and climbed up and down for sixteen miles to Chapulhuacanito (Chap-pul-wha-can-eato), our destination.

The sun beat down mercilessly as we traveled along the open spaces, however, there were also long stretches of shade when the path led through miles of forest. Giant tropical cedars, huge oaks, rose woods and other trees spread their graceful branches over the path. Long, lovely vines hung from the trees, which had rare plants in their boughs. Tall ferns and a profusion of plants grew along the roadside, often hanging over a stony cliff. At places the path grew rugged and difficult, then again smoother and wider in spots.

All along the way, there were crosses in memory of the many travelers who had died in those spots in fights and robberies, for there were no car accidents here. As we turned a curve where the path widened, a newer, larger cross appeared

12

around the bend. "Who is that cross for and what happened here?" I asked Don Miguel.

"Oh that is for Don Pedro, Don Julio's brother from Chapulhuacanito. He was on his way home after selling some cattle, when he was attacked, robbed and killed by a bandit gang."

"Did they get the bandits?" I asked hopefully.

"Oh, no, not those! They are very clever ones. The leader is a very much wanted man, but he is very powerful and has many friends who are willing to cover up for him. They have just returned from the Tampico area. They work several states going from one to another when the army gets too close to them."

"That must have been a very hard blow to poor Don Julio and the family," I replied.

I had heard about his brother being murdered when I was helping Doctora Dale in her clinic. He and a nephew had come to get medicine for their families, and the Doctora expressed her sympathy to them.

In my mind, I again saw this tall, distinguished, heavy-set, white-haired gentleman to whom I had felt drawn at once, as someone I would like to know better. So, I was glad when Doctora Dale introduced us.

After they left, she told me that he was the most influential man in the area where I was going to work, and the nephew who was with him, also a fine looking man, was the postmaster in Chapulhuacanito.

About noon, we came to a little stream and decided to eat our lunch and rest in the shade. Jose wasn't sure he would like our sandwiches; so he pulled out some tacos, made of corn tortillas, from his shoulder bag, called a morral, and being shy,

13

sat off to one side by himself to eat. However, Don Miguel, who had been a rural school teacher and was used to eating different foods, shared my lunch, and ate with gusto.

Soon, we heard the swift, hard beat of horses hoofs approaching, and I was somewhat relieved when a nicely dressed Spanish-type man on a good looking black steed came into view. With him were two other men on common-looking horses, probably his peones, hired men. When he saw us, he pulled in the reins, leaned over the saddle and introduced himself.

"You must be the fine young nurse who is coming to our pueblo. I am the presidente, mayor, there and I now take the privilege with pleasure of welcoming you and offering my services. My good neighbor, Don Julio, has told us how nice you are, and everybody is anxious for your coming, including my wife, who is expecting any day now. You will have a lot of work to do," he commented with a twinkle in his eye. After again putting himself "a sus ordenes," at my service, he rode away, leaving a very much-encouraged girl with a new impulse to continue the journey.

And it was nice to know that the feeling between Don Julio and myself had been mutual.

After riding for over three hours without seeing a house, we now came to the first thatched-roof mud huts just outside of our little village, which had a population of about 1000 with another 1000 in the "suburbs" around it.

As we entered, there was a fork in the road. Standing to one side of it was a rather large wooden cross in front of a low moss-covered stone wall. On the other side of the wall was a coffee grove with its graceful frijolio trees giving just the right amount of shade needed for the coffee bushes. There were no houses nearby, and the weather-beaten cross, with a lovely string of yellow flowers entwined around it, stood like a lonely sentinel to receive weary travelers when they arrived.

Here Don Miguel parted ways with us for he was going further on to preach in another village that night.

In order to get to our Indian compound, we made a right-hand turn going down a little path. Soon, we arrived at Jose's house, where his wife Juana sat on the doorstep embroidering a colorful cross-stitch blouse like the one she was wearing, typical of their northern Aztec tribe. From another hut in the same patio, Jose's brother, Mauro, hurried to greet us, followed by a group of giggling boys. Peering timidly from the doorway in the background was his sister, Maria, just a wisp of a girl about twelve or thirteen, motherless and unhappy. Also, sitting nearby was his father with a fixed smile, which caused him to look suspiciously senile. After passing a few more huts, from which came other smiling people greeting us, we came to the spot which was to be home for the next few years.

"Buenas tardes, Señorita. Where have you been so long? We had dinner ready for you. Seemed you would never arrive," beamed plump, dimpled Lola, and pretty bashful Andrea, the girls who were to be my companions. As we embraced, Andrea's family and other neighbors came to give me a hearty welcome.

Now, the girls helped to carry the things into our house, which had been built for us by the kind Indian brethren right behind the church. There was only a passage between. Our home was a long mud hut with a thatched roof, but it was nicely plastered and white-washed. It had been divided into four small rooms. The clinic and the living room combined was the larger, with a door and a window. The kitchen beside it was narrow with only a door and a mud stove just inside the door. At the other end towards the east, overlooking the river far below, were the two bedrooms. Each room had a window with panes and screens made by a native carpenter under Rev. Dale's direction.

The carpenter had also made native canvas cots for Lola and me, which were wider and more comfortable than army cots. They were recommended to be cooler than regular beds. That idea was all right for summer months, but even then it gets mighty chilly in the mountains towards morning. However, there was a solution to the problem, for when I had gone to Laredo, Texas, the last time, I had found among the things waiting for me a feather-tick, that is, a feather bag mattress, which had been sent to me from Pennsylvania. It was just the thing to make my cot warm and comfortable; so I decided to bring it back from Tamazunchale the first time I went there for supplies.

In my bedroom was the only piece of presentable furniture in the house. It was a desk of cedar wood which I had a carpenter make in Tamazunchale. Also, there was my father's antique trunk which gave the room a homey feeling. Jose and Mauro had brought these things and a few straight chairs out earlier. There was also a pretty folding screen in the corner, which was very necessary for privacy when changing or bathing. Now, the only things needed were wooden clothes closets and cupboards, one for the medicines in the clinic and another with screens for the kitchen, in which to keep the food safe from rats, mice and flies. Lola said the carpenter was coming in the morning for the measurements. He had already made a table for the kitchen and benches for the clinic.

Outside the clinic window and the kitchen door, the

public path ran parallel with the house and the side of the church. On the other side of the path was the patio of Andrea's house, which faced ours and was much too close for bad nerves. Andrea's mother had tuberculosis. She coughed day and night, coming out to the doorway to spit and spit. It was evident that there would be little privacy at this end of the house, for everybody who went by took a glance in the window. And the boys played "peeping tom" as a new entertainment. In fact, a window was quite a new thing in their community.

At the other end of the large thatched-roof church was the property of the chief of our community, Don Domingo Grande*, who was Andrea's uncle. His house was the same type as the rest, only bigger. The kitchen was a separate, smaller house nearby. This is the common way to cook in rural Mexico. His home distinguished itself in that it sat on a higher level, and its spacious grounds had banana trees and coffee bushes. We had to climb a stone wall to reach that level.

His nephew, Don Domingo Chico*, lived on the other side of Andrea. He was the chief's right-hand man, for he spoke Spanish, which the older man did not. He understood and perhaps could have spoken it, but I was to learn soon that he did not want to identify himself with anything Spanish. Nor did he like any progress or change, wanting no contact with the world outside his own. He and his family wore only the dress of the Indian man, a white pajama-like suit, while young Domingo and the more progressive men wore blue jeans and store-bought shirts. The chief was a thin man with a narrow face and small shrewd eyes. While his nephew was a nice pleasant looking young man with a beautiful Indian wife, and

*See Glossary, pages 173-174

three lovely little children.

The older man seldom projected himself as a leader preferring to use his nephew as a front in public. But he wanted to control everything.

As night shadows fell over our little village, Andrea lit the kerosene lamp on the wall, and we had our supper and devotions.

These sweet girls were no strangers to me. Lola, who was from Tamazunchale, and I had worked together helping Doctora Dale before she, Lola, had come to this village a few months earlier. She was a graduate of their Bible School and a choice native missionary. Besides the regular church work, her special assignment here was to teach the adults to read and write. Andrea was in the Dales' home for Indian girls, going to grade school when I had arrived in Tamazunchale less than two years before. I had liked both of them very much, admiring their lovely big brown eyes, glossy braids and graceful, gentle ways.

As the soft lamplight cast flickering shadows on the rafters and the wall, a feeling of contentment came at having reached my destination, and having such nice companions with whom to live and work.

They, together with all those already mentioned and others, would be fitting into the drama of life as it would unfold within the next few years in our small spot here in the heart of Mexico.

CHAPTER

2

Dawn had arrived! The Catholic church bells were ringing, roosters were crowing, and it was time to get up. Slipping out from under my mosquito net, I went to the window. What a magnificent sight met my eyes! The clouds that enshrouded the high mountains in the distance were now serenely rising as with dignity, floating away to join others, while the first rays of sun shone through from the open spaces here and there. I hurried to get outside as soon as possible to watch the miracle of morning. The mist was rising from the gurgling creek that had lulled me to sleep the night before and sunlight soon began to dance on the ripples.

Lola came out to join me and to explain the main part of our town, which lay in the valley on the other side of the creek.

"That large cobblestone oblong town square is where market will be held tomorrow," she informed me.

"Where is the post office?" I asked, thinking of the postmaster I had met in the clinic in Tamazunchale.

"The house on the right of the cobblestone plaza, the one with the two flaming orange-colored flamboyen trees in front of it," was Lola's answer. "And that is Don Julio's house down at the other end."

"You mean the big stone one with the unfinished windows in the second story?" I asked. "I wonder why they haven't finished it."

"Well, it's not for lack of money, I'm sure," she chuckled. "People say it is because his wife doesn't want to live here. She is his second wife and somewhat younger than he is. When he married her, she was the belle of Tamazunchale. Her father was mayor at the time. She has never liked living in this out-of-the-way place; and although she is a very pleasant person, she holds herself aloof from the people here. She is always talking about the day Don Julio will retire and they will go to live in Tamazunchale."

"And those two large native-type houses on the hill just opposite us?"

"The one beside the graveyard is the temporary Catholic Church. Their stone church burned down a few years ago. See the ruins in the background?"

"And the other, beside the road that leads over the hill?"

"Oh, that is the school house."

"School house!" That brought me back to earth as I remembered that I had been commissioned by the county health doctor in Tamazunchale to vaccinate the school children. He had given me the vaccine and urged me to persuade the Indian children not in school to be vaccinated also.

When I mentioned this to Lola, she said that the school teacher had been asking for and expecting me.

By this time, others had joined us. Some had come for treatment. One, a sweet Christian widow, Doña Linda, spoke good Spanish. She had just arrived from the state of Hidalgo with her young sons because of persecution there. In her arms she held a pathetic-looking little boy whose big swollen legs dangled from a very thin little body. It looked as though he had elephantiasis, but instead it was a very bad case of pernicious anemia brought on by chronic malaria. We would do all we could for him, I assured her, but she realized that only a miracle would save him. She offered to do my laundry, as she needed work badly. And I was glad to let her do it, down at the creek, as all our water had to be carried up the hill from there. Doña Linda and I were to become close friends as we tried to help each other in the years I would be living there.

That afternoon more callers arrived. Don Julio's daughter, Lilia, came with her Aunt Lyla. Lilia was in her teens and a very sweet outgoing girl. When she introduced herself, and we exchanged names, a Mexican custom, she said that her nickname was "La Chata," which means snubnose.

"What do they call you in your home?" she asked me.

"They just call me Mae," I replied.

"Then that is what we will call you at our house, Mae." And she pronounced it correctly, which was surprising, as most Mexicans don't, so that I prefer their using the Mexican interpretation, Maria.

The special reason for their visit was to bring me an invitation from Lilia's mother and father for dinner on Thursday. "We would like to have you come tomorrow, but it is market day, you know," Lilia said.

Market day, I had heard that so often I was getting quite excited about it myself.

As we said "goodbye" outside my door, it seemed that dark, resentful looks came from the direction of Andrea's house, and I realized that Andrea had indeed disappeared very quickly when my visitors had arrived. I wondered about this.

Late in the afternoon, we noticed a lot of hustle and bustle in the town square below us. Mules, donkeys and horses were arriving with the merchandise. The merchants were putting up poles on which they stretched canvas roofs. They were preparing to sleep there by their goods in order to have their displays ready early the next morning. These traveling merchants go from one town to another for market days, held each week. There was also a lot of squealing and commotion, as the pigs and steers were being butchered. Market day was the only day in the week that we could buy meat.

Lola and I brought a small bench out to sit and watch the active scene below. But there was another scene, just as fascinating, above it all. The clouds that had floated away in the morning, were coming back to cover the mountains for the night, hovering over the highest peak, which was in the shape of the oblong sail of a galley ship. The clouds were now rose-tinted by the reflection of the setting sun. The mountains were also changing color from different shades of blue to luminous purple as they, too, reflected the setting sun. We sat intrigued until the sun went down. I'm going to get out my easel and oils and paint this view sometime, I decided. The picture now hangs on the wall in my study.

The next morning there were early visitors, mostly Indian men from the next village, wanting medicine to take back to their sick. One wanted salve for his boy who had been bitten by a dog, fortunately not a mad dog. By the time I finished with the last patient it was later than we had hoped. Now we hurriedly picked up our baskets and bags to go to market for our weekly supplies.

As we crossed the creek, hopping from one stepping stone to another, I remarked, "This creek really divides the town, running right through the middle of it."

"Yes it really does, in more ways than one," replied Lola. "It separates the Indian and the Spanish-speaking people.

Therefore, whichever side you live on is the wrong side to the people in the opposite direction."

So I had not been mistaken when I thought I saw dislike and resentment in Andrea and her family when Don Julio's daughter Lilia had come to call. Well, one thing is certain I thought to myself, I am going to be a friend of all to the best of my ability, regardless of what problems it might bring. And maybe I could even help to bridge the gulf, somehow.

When we reached the post office, which was also a little store, I entered to greet the postmaster, Señor Flores, who introduced me to his wife. She held a baby in her arms while another little one was hanging on to his daddy, who patted his head and caressed him. Seeing how devoted he was to his family was really impressive.

The market was indeed interesting with its many kinds of stands, clothing, yardage goods, notions, kitchenware, baskets and whatnots, most of which were spread out on cloth on the ground. I bought a few clay flower pots with Indian designs, which we filled with vegetables. How glad I was to see potatoes! There were also tomatoes, onions, etc. The meat hanging up in the open air was covered by flies. And there were skinny, squawking chickens to buy from Indian men and women, squatting behind their little piles of vegetables or whatever they had to offer.

La Chata waved to us as we passed her house, and most of the people were very friendly. So, as we climbed up the steep curving hillside in the hot sun with our pots, bags, and baskets full, I decided that market day was indeed all I had anticipated it to be.

When we arrived, there were more patients waiting for

us, and I worked on into the late afternoon. Tonight was the mid-week service, and there was a portable folding organ which it was my privilege to play. It had to be pumped by foot, and the lamps were quite dim, but it was soothing to play the hymns in the soft lamplight. Don Domingo Chico gave the message standing by a small table. Indian brethren sat on one side, and the women on the other side on simple benches, singing with much enthusiasm, for this was one way they had of expressing themselves.

Inside the church there was much reverence and devotion, but outside was another matter. Most of the young men hadn't come in, while others had slipped outside before the preaching started. Now they were whispering, giggling, and chasing each other around the church. At first it wasn't so bad, but as they gained momentum, restraint was forgotten, and they became a band of whooping Indians as their bare, stamping feet went faster, around and around.

Don Domingo Grande went out and scolded them, so they settled down. His own boys and Andrea's brothers, his nephews, were the ring-leaders. A few came in and sat down for awhile, but they soon became restless and left to join their companions; so the whole performance started all over again. On one of their trips through the passage way between our house and the church, there was a big crash — the flower pots I had bought at the market and which we had lugged up the steep hill!

We should put a gate at this passageway, I mused, and decided to suggest this to Don Domingo Chico. Also, having a high bamboo fence at the other side of the church would be nice, so we could have flowers in the little patio and more privacy.

When the gate and fence were made, everyone was

relieved and happy except those young men. We got some dark, defiant looks from the direction of their hangouts, the stone wall and the banana grove beside Andrea's house.

The visit to Don Julio's house was indeed pleasant. La Chata and her mother were looking for me at the open door. Her mother greeted me saying, "You are Mae. I'm glad to have you with us, and I hope that you will feel that our house is your house — 'Mi casa es su casa.' "

When she said that her name was Aurora Hervert, I thought Aurora would be a difficult name for my new Spanish.

"Aurora means Dawn in your language," La Chata offered, "And my father says that our last name, Hervert, would be Herbert in English."

Doña Dawn was a petite little lady with a mass of black wavy hair piled up on her head so that she looked quite aristocratic. It was cool in the large, well-ventilated room and the dinner table looked inviting. But since the men hadn't come in from supervising the sugar cane fields yet, Doña Dawn now introduced me to her family by the pictures on the wall. There was one of her father and mother, his father and mother and their own wedding pictures, all in antique oval frames. The most outstanding was a lovely new elegant picture of their oldest daughter, who had been married just the year before to a lawyer. She was a beautiful bride, and what a costly exquisite gown she wore! Doña Dawn said that Don Julio had insisted that she be married here in the village, and it was a tremendous wedding. The judge, priest, musicians, relatives and friends had to come from town on horseback. It was the biggest affair the place ever had and cost them thousands of pesos. "But," she commented, "these things only happen once in a lifetime."

There were four children in the family. Lilia, La Chata, the youngest, then her brother, Luis, who helped his father with the ranch. But any one could see that the one who gave Doña Dawn the most pride and joy was her oldest son, Marcos. "He is studying in Mexico City and is preparing to be a doctor," she stated with satisfaction. He certainly was handsome and intelligent looking, resembling his father, yet having his mother's sensitive mouth and some of her fine features.

"I'm sure he will be a very good doctor," I agreed, as she told me how wonderful he was. But at the time he was only a picture on the wall, as far as I was concerned.

Now, we heard the beat of horses hoofs, as Don Julio and his son came riding across the cobblestones toward the house, while we all went to the door to wave a welcome.

The dinner was delicious, and the conversation and atmosphere very pleasant. There was no doubt that this was a happy and devoted family. As we finished, Doña Dawn casually pushed a napkin toward Don Julio's hand, but he just as casually pushed it away, then lifted the corner of her exquisite tablecloth and wiped his mustache with it. Whereupon she just turned up an eyebrow with an "It's no use" expression on her face and a twinkle in her eye.

As Doña Dawn excused herself to clear the table, Don Julio really began to talk. He told me he had fought in the revolution for liberty of religion and separation of church and state and considered himself, in a way, one of us Evangelicos, Protestants*, instead of a Catholic. However, he believed that all religion was good for people if they didn't get fanatical about it.

"My mother and sisters are fanatical," he said. "But my wife isn't. She is also a devoted Catholic, but I don't let her get

*See Glossary, pages 173-174

carried away. She lives her religion, has her prayers in her bedroom, and isn't out gossiping about her neighbors.

"I helped your religion come to these parts," he informed me. "It was through my good friend, Don Martin, who was quite a preacher. I took him around to the villages and introduced him, and he preached to the crowds that gathered. He had a terrific personality and a silver tongue and could really influence people.

"One time he came out here when they were having a fiesta at the Catholic Church, which later burned down. We went to see what was going on. They were having an Indian dance in the church yard, and there was gambling, drinking, and carousing all around the place. Finally, Don Martin could stand it no longer so he climbed up on something and started to preach. That sure was a shock and took the life out of the fiesta.

"The next morning, before we got up, here came practically all the women of the town, with my mother and sisters in the front, clamoring for Don Martin. They were carrying a plank and some rope, yelling that they were going to tie him on it and put him under water, until he came to his senses and repented of his heresy. I begged him not to open the door. 'It's better to talk to them from the window,' I suggested. 'You are a gentleman and can't fight women. Although you are a big vigorous man, you will be the loser.'

"But he would not listen to me, Señorita Mae, saying, 'Open the door and I'll reason with them.' So he stepped up to the open door and said, 'Buenos días, Señoras, what has brought you out so early?' 'Because you are sacreligious, and you desecrated our church last night. You will repent or pay for what you did,' they yelled at him. 'I am very sorry about the way you feel, but wait just a minute,' he reasoned. 'Let me tell you something first. It was you and your husbands and sons who were desecrating your church with your carousing, drinking, dancing, gambling, cursing and all that was going on there. As for me, I was only doing what is supposed to be done in churches, I was preaching God's Word, The Gospel, God's message for sinners to repent. It was you and your families who were profaning your church with the like of the things you were doing there.' The women just looked at each other and backed off, then broke up into groups and disappeared. That man! He could just about convince anyone, even me," Don Julio added.

"And what happened that you didn't continue?" I asked impulsively.

At this question, he became reserved and replied in a measured voice, "Maybe I will tell you someday, when there is more time." But I knew he meant, when I know you better.

Chagrined, I turned the conversation back to a less personal channel, "What happened to Don Martin and where is he now? I would enjoy meeting him."

"Well, for one thing, he got interested in politics and ran for Mayor in Tamazunchale. But, he lost, got a bad deal in my opinion, so he left these parts. The last I heard he was in Tampico.

"It was about that time that the Dales came and their son Johnny learned Aztec perfectly. Because of this and the Doctora's medicines, they have had great success with the Indians. It is marvelous how they have won the confidence and hearts of the Indians, which we Mexicans have been unable to do. They have built the church here and many other churches, but they are Indian churches, not for us Mexicans. The Indians don't want us, and we can't blame them for they know that if the Spanish-speaking come into their churches, they will soon take over the leadership, and they, the Indians, would take the back seat. So, it's all right this way. It's their show; let them run it. They need religion more than we do for they need to get civilized and educated."

We talked a little more about things in general, especially the war news which was anything but good in those early days of '41. Before leaving, they suggested that I come to listen to the six o'clock news on their radio whenever possible. I was glad to accept the invitation, because except for letters, this would be my only contact with the outside world.

CHAPTER

3

Days seemed to go racing by in this land of horses, and interesting things were seen and learned each day as I journeyed in this strange, fascinating land of which so much was new to me.

The date had been set to vaccinate the school children. So I climbed the steep hill opposite us, on the other side of the creek to the little thatched roof school house which stood in front of the graveyard near the Catholic Church.

The school teacher was a middle aged man with fiery black eyes and a black mustache. He bristled with importance and outdid himself with courtesy when I arrived.

There were only about 30 pupils, which was a small number for such a largely populated area. He explained that the Indian children wouldn't come for they were shy and out of their element. Another reason was that he spoke no Aztec and they spoke no Spanish.

"They ought to be vaccinated also Señorita," he advised. "Why don't you have them come to your house on a special day? That is the only way it can be done, for they will not come to this side of the town."

So Lola and I set a date, and to our surprise a long line of Indian children and young people lined up outside the clinic on the appointed afternoon to be vaccinated. The older ones were giggling and a few little ones were crying. Lola passed them on to me, and Andrea interpreted in Aztec, telling them not to scratch the sore, nor to go bathing in the creek until well. We all hoped they understood the seriousness of these instructions, but that was really a lot to expect.

Even the Indian grown-ups were like children. One would come with a high fever, then go bathing or wash clothes in the creek the very next day and complain that the medicine didn't work. Or they would be sick enough to be in bed with next thing to pneumonia, then come to church in the rain, with their scanty clothing soaked to the skin. Nor did the Indians believe in germs or contagion. And since they didn't want to believe, nor hear about these things, it was going to take a lot of patience on the part of this new "germ-conscious" nurse. Instead of germs, their idea was that there were evil spirits in the air or in certain houses, which caused them to get sick. Looking back, I wonder if maybe it all added up to more or less the same thing, germs.

A few weeks after the vaccinations, a very sick boy finally came for help. He had a very high fever and a big hole in his arm.

"Why haven't you come before?" I asked Pedro, a skinny boy of about fourteen.

"Because my stepmother didn't want me to. She and her friend the 'Curandera,' lady witch doctor, have been putting things on it."

"Things like what?" I asked.

"Oh, leaves, mud packs and such things."

"You must have scratched it or gone in the creek to have become infected like this."

"Oh, yes, I bathed in the creek, but the water was clear

and clean, so it wasn't that. It was because I ate an egg, and a little bit of chicken, too, and they have evil spirits in them, you know."

While I thought their ways strange, they also found mine odd to them. When I gave a woman with a fever a warm sponge bath, she would protest asking, "Why hot water when I am already hot? Cold water would feel so much better." And there was the woman who was to take a laxative. She objected, saying, "But I can't take that now." When I asked her why, she replied, "Because it isn't the right time of the moon." Another woman, who had taken a purge we hadn't prescribed, sent her daughter to ask if she could dare go to sleep, because she was so sleepy and could hardly stay awake. Being puzzled, Lola enlightened me that it was supposedly dangerous to sleep after taking a purge or a laxative.

Every morning, the clinic was full of hopeful patients, mostly poor, who brought a few centavos, eggs, a squash or something to show their appreciation. But, also, there were others of more means, who often brought their injections prescribed by the doctors in town to simply be applied. Some of my patients, especially the Indian brethren from the villages beyond, I already knew, for they had come to the clinic of Doctora Dale in Tamazunchale, while I was helping her there.

One of them was the Indian brother from the village of Laguna, twenty-some miles away. He had brought his son who had been bitten by a dog. This fine looking man and his nice young brother were new Believers. They lived in a very fanatical territory on the other side of San Felipe, farther on beyond us in the backward, fanatical state of Hidalgo. Their lives were constantly threatened by their neighbors and the men of San Felipe.

Another of my patients was a young school teacher from up in the mountains across the state line of Hidalgo which was just a few miles away. He brought his baby and others to be treated, was very frail himself and had a bad cough. He, Professor Leo, liked our teaching, the Bible reading and prayers we had in the clinic each morning. He had gone to a Protestant school in the state and city of Queretaro. But, he was very secretive about his interest in the Gospel, not wanting anyone to know. He told us of school teachers he had known, who were considered too liberal-minded, and who were run out of their schools and even killed by the "Sinarquists," a fanatical Fascist group, with their flaming crosses on the hillsides and their cries of death to the Protestants. They marched by night on churches or into homes to burn and to kill. This same Fascist group, also called Cristeros, was using their propaganda against the United States, trying to align the Mexican people with the Fascist countries during these early days of World War II. This was evident when I went to listen to the radio at Don Julio's or when I had the chance to read the newspaper.

Professor Leo would ask for Christian literature to take home to read, then he would safely hide it away inside his shirt for no one to see. He also asked for seeds for a garden, as he was anxious to show his students how to plant and raise vegetables. I had a few on hand to give him, and promised to get him more on my next trip to Tamazunchale for supplies.

The lesser cases at the clinic were wounds, old sores and ulcers, sore eyes, malaria, digestive disturbances and worms. One little fellow with a big stomach passed 52 worms after treatment.

The more pathetic sights met my eyes when out calling in the homes. People were dying of T.B., malaria, anemia and dysentery, often with very little care or food, just wasting away. Some of them could be helped and brought back to health, others were not so fortunate, but in every case they could be prayed for and given the assurance of eternal life in Christ, after this vale of suffering. Fortunately, most of them wanted this kind of help. One sweet elderly lady lying on the floor in a pile of dirty clothes was covered with ants, lice and flies. On the second visit, I took a change of clothes along and clean newspapers. After the first bath which she had in months and while lying on nice clean newspapers, she accepted Christ as her personal Savior. Her face lit up with joy, as she exclaimed, "Now I shall die very happy." It wasn't long afterward that the Lord took her to the mansions beyond.

Often on my rounds, I would carry some unusual equipment besides my medical bag, such as soap and towels, jars of soup, newspapers and sometimes a spray gun for disinfecting.

Sometimes by night, I was so tired I felt like just dropping into bed, but going to bed wasn't as simple as that in this place.

All day long I had been out collecting fleas in my clothing, little wee things, hard to see and harder yet to catch and to kill. Often I would find some twenty in the seams of my clothing, having to part them with my fingernails to be sure they were dead, but some always got away.

Finally, in desperation, I started to undress in the darkened clinic, throwing my clothes as far away as possible, rolling up my pajama legs and racing for the cot, hoping that I hadn't picked up any hitch hikers as I jumped into bed and tucked the mosquito net in tight. It was at this time that I learned to say my evening prayers in bed. And back to those awful fleas; some always found me during the night, so I wore out many flash-light batteries hunting them. It wasn't the bites that bothered so much as their constant jumping around. I used to think, why don't they get filled up like mosquitos do, then go away and leave a person in peace.

This wasn't the only unpleasant problem we had. A really big one was that there was no toilet and no place to put one on our tiny lot. So we had to do like the rest of the people did — go up to the hill, past Andrea's house, then past her cousin's house, cross a mule path, and climb over a stone fence to a coffee grove which was the public out-house. There was no house, but it was sure "out," and what a filthy place! It was hard to wade through, where no one had sat before, to a cleaner spot beyond. And there was always the suspense that one would bump into another's privacy, or be intruded upon by someone else. However, somehow, that never happened, perhaps because the Indians are children of the forest and know how to vanish unseen. In dry, hot weather it was bad enough, but when it rained, it got slimy as well, and the stench of it became worse.

Lola and I often wondered what could be done. One possibility was that the people who owned the lot next to us would rent it to us. However, we knew that Dr. Dale had tried to buy that lot to build our house up there in the open breeze instead of on the small plot of gound next to the church, but the owners wouldn't sell. So we had little hope that they would even rent it to us, but we did start to pray.

These were the experiences which weren't so romantic and often after a sleepless night or a trip up that hill, I had to take a good long look at those lofty distant mountains to get above it all.

Early one morning a face appeared at my bedroom window. I never did get used to being awakened in this unusual manner. The poor man seemed distraught as he pleaded, "Señorita, won't you come and help my woman before she dies. I have been waiting long hours for daylight to come before calling on you," he explained. "My wife has been in labor for over two days and now she has no strength left to give birth."

Grabbing my obstetrical satchel, I hurried after him, down the path on our side of the creek to a part of the village new to me. On the dirt floor of a little Indian hut, was the sick woman with several Indian women gathered around her.

Upon examination, I found that her problem was a breech birth. When I just touched her abdomen she cringed with pain. Those women had pushed and punched her, trying to get that baby out, until she was very sore. The child still had heart beats but very faint, and the mother was indeed very weak, to put it mildly.

After explaining the situation and encouraging her that everything would be all right, with God's help, I gave her some coffee and a wine and iron tonic. This put a little more life into her and put everyone else in a brighter sprit.

With clean newspapers underneath and a clean sheet over her, I began the delivery. It was not difficult to reach those little feet, which come first in these cases. Soon the baby was born, limp as a rag, which is the usual condition in these long drawn out breech cases. He responded to a little shaking and spanking, giving his first weak little cry which brought a happy gasp from the father and a wane smile from the mother. Everyone got happy all of a sudden. They could not thank me enough, and the proud father gave me a chicken for my pay.

The next evening, Don Domingo Chico came with a big

smile on his face. We invited him in and after small talk, as is their custom, he finally got around to saying, "I bring you good news. The father of the baby you delivered yesterday is very grateful and says that, but for you, the mother and the baby would have died. Now, what I have to tell you will make you very happy. You see, he is a part-owner of the land next to you. It is an inheritance which they have not been able to settle between themselves. But he talked to his brothers, and they are all willing that you may use the plot for whatever you wish, without paying anything, except that you can't put a house on it. However, you can build a chicken house, or a shelter for cattle or whatever else you wish.

Wonderful! That would mean we would have our much needed out-house. The problem was solved; our prayers had been answered.

That night I was so happy when I went to bed that I didn't mind the jumping fleas, barking dogs, or the coughing neighbors. Instead, I was dreaming of our new toilet of bamboo, with it's thatched roof, built at just the right spot among the trees. I would plant morning glory vines beside it. We would put a gate in the fence of the patio leading up to it. The gate would be painted blue, and I would plant roses and flowering vines along the fence.

CHAPTER

4

Since it seemed that I was well settled Lola decided it was time to go to visit her family in town. She needed the rest and change, so she was gone for a week.

The house seemed lonesome without her. Sometimes in the evening I went to Don Domingo Chico's house to sit with his family around their fire on the floor, holding their little baby girl. And in the afternoon on my way home from sick calls, I often stopped to visit with Don Julio and Doña Dawn. Then there was dear Andrea who came in the morning to start the wood fire; and in the evening to have the lamp lit for me when I arrived at dusk. Also, there were so many people coming and going that I was seldom alone.

When Lola returned she brought the bad news that our Doctora was not at all well. Her heart condition was worse. Lola had tears in her eyes when she told me, then said, "She misses you Señorita, and wants you to come in as soon as you can."

So I planned to go the next day. I had intended to go soon anyway, for there were supplies to get and I was ready for a break from it all.

Lola offered to take care of the clinic and some of the patients while I was gone. She was anxious to learn nursing as she was discouraged trying to teach women to read who did not want to learn. She could already give injections and prescribe some of the medicines.

When I told her that Don Julio offered to lend me a horse to go to town, she informed me that Rev. Dale had already asked Jose to bring me in on his donkey. So that was it! But now that we had a place to put a horse, I intended to ask Rev. Dale about the possibility of my getting one. Domingo Chico had already said it was all right with him, but he admitted that some of the older Indian brethren would not like it. It was another prejudice. The donkey identified a person with the Indian and horses with the Spanish-speaking.

However, I needed a horse to call on the sick, for many lived on the outskirts of town. I had never been a good hiker nor a climber of hills of which there were many. Also a horse was needed to go on the Evangelistic trips to the churches in other villages, and for the trips to town. Many times Don Julio lent me one of his horses, or one of the brethren would offer a donkey for the trips to other churches. But sometimes in an emergency nothing was available.

It just didn't seem reasonable that here I was in a land where horses were a way of travel, and I was without one of my own. So I couldn't help hoping.

It was sad to see our dear vibrant Doctora looking so sick. She was getting around, but did not have the clinic open. The family was living under the tension that a heart attack would come again at any time. One night they called me out of bed to give her an injection. This was the last time I was to see our beloved Doctora, for the next time I went to Tamazunchale, she had already been taken to the Hospital in San Antonio, where she died. Dr. Katherine Neel Dale was indeed a great and highly esteemed missionary, who had spent her life serving the Mexican people of her generation. Because of her loving devotion to everyone, she was in return very much loved. Two biographies have been written of her life.

Time went fast in town and the day Jose returned for me it was noon before I was ready to leave, and that made for a very late start.

"It will be dusk before we arrive home," he commented with concern.

"All right, shall we wait until tomorrow?" I asked hopefully.

"No, I have to work in the fields tomorrow, better we go today," he decided.

Crossing on the ferry was always exciting, and riding in the shade of the big overspreading trees was pleasant. But the long stretch of hot sun which followed was tiring. Finally we entered the woods where it was rougher going, but a bit cooler.

It was about then that we heard horses galloping up from behind us, together with boisterous laughter and loud coarse talking. They sounded like they had been drinking and we hoped they would pass by without noticing us. Soon they came in sight, three well-dressed men on fine horses. One was a young man whom we learned later was a school teacher. He was the guide for the other two middle-aged, heavy-set, dominant Mexicans of the Pancho Villa type, wearing expensive leather jackets and boots.

As they overtook us one of them reigned up his steed beside my little donkey and tried to start a conversation. There was no doubt now that he had been drinking. "An Americana," he exclaimed. Then boasted, "I am from the

Texas border. I can speak much English, and I have a lot of American girl friends. What is a young girl like you doing out here in the sticks?" he questioned.

"I am a missionay nurse and I am here to help the people." I answered, hoping this would cause some respect and restraint. But the effort was lost on him.

"Where is your husband, aren't you married? How about going for a little ride with me in the woods? I will pay you ten dollars," he propositioned.

Acting as though I did not understand I answered, "This burro is not for sale, Señor."

"She doesn't understand you, pal," the other man said.

"Oh, yes, she does, she is just acting dumb. We shall see."

Then he offered fifteen dollars, yelling red-faced, "I mean dollars, not pesos, dollars!"

By that time I was getting so scared I couldn't speak; so I just shook my head "No" in reply, as I scanned the horizon in vain hoping that other travelers would appear. Inside I was sure praying.

"All right!" he shouted angrily as he leaned over toward me. "I will make you one more offer, twenty dollars. How about that?"

Then, as I again shook my head trying to edge my donkey away, he drew out his revolver and shaking it at my head with his unsteady hand, threatened, "If you don't go for the good, you will go for the bad. How about it compañero?" he asked the other man, "Are you with me?"

"It's okay with me whatever you want to do. I'll go along with it," he replied.

I glanced at Jose, his face was as gray as ashes. He knew as well as I did that the first bullet would probably be for him, to silence him forever. Men like these could shoot an Indian as easily as they would a dog.

Still no other travelers appeared on the scene, but God had help even nearer. The young guide began to edge his horse between me and the menacing man who was now trying to grab me.

"Come along my friend," he advised. "There is no time to fool with women. It is getting late. You have no idea how dangerous it is in these hills at sundown. We have a long way to go, and if we get caught by a bandit gang we will all be dead men."

"That's right," agreed the spineless one, "We really don't have the time, better listen to him, compañero, he knows what he's talking about."

All the while the young man was prodding the man's horse from behind, putting distance between us. So the drunken man went, protesting loudly, but he went.

Now Jose and I conferred, shall we go on or turn back? But realizing how God had solved the problem and cared for us, we decided to go on and arrived safely home at dusk.

But Jose and his brother now made it known that they could no longer be hired to accompany me on any more trips.

When I told Don Julio about those men, he exclaimed, "That settles it. You must always use a horse of mine or get one of your own. If you want to buy one you can pasture it with mine. That way you can go and come to town with other people going on horses which will be safer."

Now Rev. Dale consented to my having a horse, and a friend in Colorado, cowboy evangelist Harvey Springer, who loved horses sent me thirty dollars toward buying one. So we started to look for just the right horse.

One of Don Julio's nephews sold me a nice Indian pony

for about thirty dollars. He was not tall, but was fast, had a good gait, and liked to jump little streams instead of wading through them, for which reason his former owner named him "Rabbit." I renamed him "Pablo," Paul, for I expected him to take me on many missionary journeys, as he did.

On these future trips an older brother of the church volunteered to accompany me. Don Segundo, whose name means second in English, was part Spanish and spoke Spanish better than anyone else in the congregation. Before he was converted, Don Segundo was the chief Indian dancer of the village, taking his band of dancers to all the religious and social festivals for many miles around in that region.

Don Segundo was a philosopher at heart, and made a good guide. He taught me many things about the Indian people, their ways, customs, and thinking.

But the only one I could talk English to for weeks and months at a time was Pablo the horse. He understood it just as well as Spanish, and made a good companion. Nor did I need to be embarrassed to ride with people who had bigger, finer horses, for mine always wanted to be right out in the lead.

CHAPTER

5

Professor Leo was still coming regularly and he looked much better, had put on a little weight and his cough was gone. One day he said, "The children of my school have never been vaccinated. Why not plan to come up and do it? Also a lot of sick people are asking for 'The Señorita' to come."

Now that I had a horse, I couldn't very well refuse, so I said, "Fine, we will plan to come as soon as I get more serum in Tamazunchale. Would there be an opportunity to give the Gospel to the village as a whole?" I asked, remembering that he was afraid of people knowing about his faith, and mine. So I was surprised when he answered, "Oh, yes, besides talking and praying in the homes, you could give a story to the children in the school. Only we would not dare to sing, for then it could be considered a religious service."

"Well, I could give a chalk talk or two on the blackboard. Wouldn't that be considered educational?"

"Yes, and I will be preparing the way by conditioning the people in the meantime. I'm sure you'll want to see how nicely my garden is doing." Then, upon leaving he took medicine and salve for different ones who could not come to the clinic. How different he seemed now, so full of enthusiasm, and confidence.

When I told Don Segundo of our conversation, he said that the village was not far and he would go with me, and that if we went early in the morning there would be no problem of getting back before nightfall. The only difficulty was the hard climb. It was up over rocky ledges until one reached the plateau where he said one felt the difference of higher altitude, a much cooler climate.

That alone sounded very attractive for it sure was hot in our valley at that time of the year.

It was a promising day when I packed my medicine bag, taking the usual supply of boiled water and a lunch. But since we were to be back early I didn't take a flashlight, sweater, nor even an "all-purpose" towel to be used at times for a pillow case, a quick bath or a head covering.

It was hard going for the horse. We stopped when almost up the mountainside at a little spring where there were nice boulders to sit on. Don Segundo, who was walking, took a rest, and I also stretched my bones from the tedious saddle ride. Then we climbed the rest of the way to a lovely smooth plateau from where we could see for miles. At this spot we could view three states; our own San Luis Potosi, then a few miles to the east, Vera Cruz, and just ahead, Hidalgo which we were now entering. The view consisted of mountains and more mountain ranges piling up one in back of the other in all directions and in all shades of green, blue and purple, with no sign of civilization in sight.

The air was so invigorating and the long straight road we crossed was very inviting. I said to Don Segundo, "I sure would like to take a gallop down that road."

He replied, "We have much work to do and the day is short; we better be on our way. Besides you know the code of these hills, Señorita, 'Do not be caught at sundown, because of the bandit gangs that roam these hills, and come forth from their hiding places looking for prey.' This nice road is one of their main drags. From here they can easily cross state border lines into safety, when pursued by the police."

So we started down the other side of the mountain and after awhile, we came to a little village nestled near the usual stream. We were given a royal welcome. The children were delighted with the chalk talks and readily lined up for vaccinations.

There beside the school house, fenced in because of the chickens and animals, was the garden, a novelty in these parts. The seeds had done well and the teacher and his children were rightfully proud of the tidy green rows of promising vegetables. But the older people thought this professor to be a little queer, raising such strange looking plants of things that were supposed to be edible. The only thing that looked familiar to them were the beans.

Everyone wanted us to come to their home for coffee and hot tortillas, and even chicken and broth.

There were many sick to treat. Along in the afternoon, Don Segundo started fussing, "That is enough. It is getting late." But there was still a dying man to pray with and a baby with an infected navel to treat. So, it was past mid-afternoon when we finally said "Adios" to the very appreciative people who had never been visited by a nurse or missionary before.

By the time we had reached the plateau again, the heat of the day was gone, and coming back to the level road we had crossed that morning, the urge for a real ride returned.

"Please, Don Segundo, let me take a gallop down that nice long road; I won't go far and won't be long."

"All right," he replied, "but be back pronto. You see the

sun is already setting, and it would be very difficult for the horse to pick his way down the mountain in the dark, and remember what I told you this morning about the bandits."

So I took off. Even the horse seemed to like the idea of an easy road for a change. We flew on and on, enjoying the top of the world. Then we started back, still galloping, when I finally began to wonder where that tiny crossroad was. Had we missed it? Where was Don Segundo anyway? These crossroads were really only little paths, all looking alike. Trying one then another, I soon realized that I was lost. It was indeed dusk, but darkness was coming on faster as a storm had started to brew. The sky grew black, and the wind started to blow cold and penetrating. Here I was, chilled to the bone without even a towel for protection, no flashlight as it became darker, and no house within miles. Then a new fear came upon me as I remembered what Don Segundo had said about bandit gangs. Perhaps one was headed this way right now. Looking around I could see no place to hide. Was that thunder I heard in the distance or was it oncoming horses' hoofs?

Finally, in desperation, I began to pray. Looking to God and putting my predicament in his hands, I grew calmer, my mind cleared and God got through with a message to let the horse take me home. Why of course, how foolish of me! Hadn't I always heard that a horse knows his way home?

Facing Pablo crossways on the road, I gave him the rein and patting his head said, "Come Pablo, let's go home." He took me by paths that seemed to be in the wrong direction, but soon we came to a spot that looked familiar; and after awhile we arrived at the spring where Don Segundo was sitting on a rock with his Indian blanket over his shoulder, reading his Bible with a flashlight.

He looked up at a very chagrined girl and said, "I knew

there was no use hunting you, so all I could do was sit here and pray that you would have the sense to let the horse bring you back."

As we picked our way slowly down the rocky slope by the help of his flashlight, he couldn't help saying, "I told you so," and added, "You kept going into all those casitas to visit and pray, when I told you it was getting late." Then he added with a chuckle, "They say those Norteamericanos always prepare so far ahead, and here you are without a wrap or a flashlight."

As we crawled and stumbled down the last stretch of the wearysome way we came to a point from which we could look down into our valley. The flickering lights of our own little village never looked more welcome, the lights of home.

At times like these, the words of an old song of by-gone days came back to me. The song was called, "When it's Lamp Lighting Time in the Valley."

Doña Dawn was giving the last polishing touches to the lamp globe when I stopped by late one afternoon several days later. She had a happy look on her face, as she blew into the glass, then rubbed it more briskly than usual. "There will be another member of our family, new to you, riding home with our men tonight."

"Really! Can it be that your son Marcos is home for a visit?"

"No, it's Julito, Don Julio's nephew and namesake."

"Oh, you mean the son of Don Pedro, who was killed."

"Yes, he has come back from his wanderings in the mountains, with an army squad in pursuit of the bandits who murdered his father. We are all so relieved to have him back safely." She sighed. "You see he has an obsession that he should avenge the death of his father. And of course the bandit knows

49

that and could lay in wait for him also. However, when he left here, his uncle made him promise that he would not separate himself from the soldiers, and that has been some consolation to his Tio Julio."

"That must have been a rough life living and riding with the soldiers. Did they have any success?"

"No, not even a skirmish. They are so clever, that gang. When the trail gets too hot, they disband and go into hiding. They have plenty of money, and have many friends to help them out. Julito says they have now gone down to the Tampico area."

The sound of returning horses interrupted our conversation. As we stood in the doorway to wave a welcome, I noticed that the good-looking, light-complexioned young man of about 18, who was riding close to his uncle was indeed thin and haggard.

"He will look different in a few days," his aunt commented, as though she had read my thoughts.

When we were introduced, young Julio was very polite, but withdrawn. However, his solicitous uncle was in a happier mood. "We'll get a little flesh on this boy, before he goes home to his mother. Did you send her that letter today, dear?" he asked Doña Dawn.

"Indeed I did! Poor woman, she'll be so relieved and happy."

Julito's mother was teaching school in the city of Valles, where her daughters, his sisters, were in school. He, too, had been in school there before the tragedy, but had spent all of his vacations here in the village with his father working on their ranch which was called "San Pedro."

In the days that followed, he and his uncle were inseparable. He had gone to visit his mother, but came right back, restless and melancholy. All this did not have a good effect on Don Julio, who also became very moody.

One day when I arrived unexpectedly at the doorway, I heard Don Julio's voice asking, "Has llegado con Dios? Tell me," he insisted, "Have you arrived with God?"

At first I was puzzled, for he was alone. Then as I stepped inside, I saw that he was sitting engrossed at a very small table, on which he had placed his hands, as he gazed off into space, not seeing me at all.

Just then, Doña Dawn appeared at the opposite door, motioning me over to her in the kitchen. "It's that Ouija board again," she complained. "He's trying to talk to his dead brother. I don't believe in it and it makes me feel very weird, but if it gives him any comfort, I can't object."

Later, when Don Julio discovered that I knew about the mysterious board, he asked me what I thought about it. "My mother says this is of the Devil and of evil spirits. What do you think?"

"I agree with your mother, Don Julio. What results have you had with it anyway?"

"Oh, I've had results. It has assured me of what I wanted to know, that my brother has arrived with God. For it has answered me 'yes.' "

"Tell me, how does it answer 'yes'? I'd like to know."

"It's the way it moves under my hands, when I ask a question. And I know it works," he declared.

"I don't deny that it works, but it probably is an evil spirit that makes it work."

"That I don't know," he admitted. "But Doña Dawn wants me to give it back to the friend who loaned it to me. So that's what I'll do, then all you women can rest in peace.

Anyway, I found out what I wanted to know. The thing that is worrying me now is that young Julio is leaving with the soldiers again, going on a wild goose chase which can come to no good end."

"Why don't you talk to him and tell him that it is God who will avenge him someday?"

"Why don't you tell him? I have talked and talked to no avail."

"I'd be glad to if I had the opportunity, but he never gives me the chance to talk to him."

"Well, we will just have to put him in God's hands," Don Julio replied, "for the soldiers will be coming for him in a day or two."

"Yes," added Doña Dawn, "we can only commit him to God. Dios es Grande!" God is Great.

CHAPTER

6

One of the girls who went gracefully tripping by the house several times a day on the way to and from the creek for water was Maria, Jose's little sister. She always looked so sad and dejected, sometimes she turned her regally held head slightly, on which was perched the water jar, and gave a little half smile when greeted. But it was sort of a cynical bitter smile with a suspicious, sad look in her eyes.

And no wonder, with a drunken father and several older brothers to cook and wash for, even though she was only a slip of a girl, about thirteen. Her mother had died and Juana, Jose's wife, who lived in the hut next to them, was supposed to be helping take care of her. But she showed no love, interest, nor helpfulness; for she was a selfish woman, always complaining about headaches and fretting over the fact that she had no children.

Instead, she had the defenseless child do her work also; while she sat on her front doorstep embroidering beautiful Aztec blouses, watching people go by on the path, and meddling in all the current gossip. Maria came to church. However, I never saw her whispering and giggling with the other girls. She always sat apart, tired and dazed.

As time went by it occurred to me one day that Maria

seemed to be growing up all of a sudden. She was filling out beneath the full blouse and wide skirt, but I suspected nothing more.

Then one night after I was already in bed, Jose came calling, "Señorita, please come, my little sister is very sick. She is screaming with pain."

"Wait until I get dressed. I will be right there," I replied.

But before we left another brother came, saying, "No need to bother the Señorita now. It is all over."

"All over, has she died?" I gulped out.

"No, she had a baby. The pain was a baby!" he stammered with excitement.

Poor Jose! He sank in a chair looking as white as the day we were threatened by those bad border Mexicans on the trail. "It can't be! It can't be!" he protested shaking his head.

"Come, we must go at once! She might die," I urged.

"Better that she did, both of them. What a disgrace to our family! Better we were all dead," he moaned, as we hurried out into the night and down the path by the rays of his lantern.

I had grabbed a bundle of newspapers, and my obstetrical bag, but in the excitement I forgot that I had put the scissors and things on the stove to sterilize them earlier in the evening.

What a sight met our eyes. In the middle of the dimly lit hut on the bare floor with nothing under him, nor over him, was a fat naked baby boy lying alone, still attached to the placenta. He was yelling at the top of his lungs about the cold reception he was getting from such a cruel world. There was a large circle of women around him, many of whom I had never seen before. They were standing there in judgement it seemed, doing nothing, when no doubt most of them had helped in times of childbirth. It was obvious that they had been fooled by Maria's wide skirts and draping rebozo.

But where was Maria? Surely a baby that young had to have a mother nearby. The poor girl had crawled into a dark secluded corner where she crouched trembling, about to go into shock. Her eyes looked like those of a hunted, trapped animal. So I spoke reassuringly to her as I rubbed her arms and forehead with alcohol. Then, getting her to lie down, I treated her and covered her with more wide skirts, placing the baby in her arms.

"Will someone please get a cup of hot coffee for Maria?" I asked. No one stirred.

It was about then that I discovered the absence of my surgical instruments to cut the cord. So, going to the kitchen for coffee, I asked Jose, who was sulking in a corner with his brothers, to please go to the house and ask Lola to send them to me.

Fortunately there was hot coffee in a pot near the flickering fire. While I was pouring it, Mauro, her brother, came up to me saying in a husky voice, "Ask her to tell us whose child that is, who did this terrible thing to her and to us. She must tell, and I will kill him, so I will."

"I will ask her, but on one condition, Mauro, that you and your brothers will do nothing rash and foolish. You know you would go to jail, and that would be much more of a disgrace on the family and all of us. Will you promise?"

"All right," he agreed, "but we must know."

When I returned to Maria there was a change in her eyes. They now had a tender protecting mother look. She was no longer alone in the world, for the bundle of humanity she held in her arms was hers. Propping her head on my knees to give

55

her sips of coffee I said, "That's a nice boy you have, Maria. Would you mind telling me who the father is?"

At first her eyes said "No." "You know he has to have a name, Maria," I continued. "You need not be afraid, nothing terrible will happen if you tell."

After hesitating a bit she murmured, "Antonio."

An extra hush fell over the place as everyone hung on the reply. "Who?" I asked, then more clearly she repeated, "Antonio." That was Juana's brother who had been living with her and Jose. The sad part of it was that he had just married another girl a few months before.

"Did you tell Antonio you were expecting a baby before he got married, Maria?"

"No," she answered.

"Why?" I asked.

"I didn't know it," she replied childlike. Of course not; she probably didn't know until it came big upon her.

About that time the room became vacant. The women slipped one by one out into the night. These curious gossiping ones had learned what they had come to find out and were now ready to spread the news. Only a few of our nearest Christian neighbors stayed and now offered to help clean up.

Juanita was not there. It was too painful! She, who so wanted a baby, and she, who should have been taking care of Maria. Perhaps she had known what was going on and what to expect.

A few days later an older brother of Maria's who was preaching in other villages came, and was equally shocked and embarrassed.

"What shall we do," he asked me when he came to the house. "Should we continue to have her and this child, a bastard in our house, when this is such a disgrace to us? Should I as the oldest brother give her a good beating? She should be punished in some way!" he added confused.

"Where would she go if you turn her out?" I reasoned. "And what would you gain? Everybody knows, and it would be cruel and unchristian. As for beating her, she is still sick and could die. Then look what a disgrace that would be! Why not just leave her to God. He always punishes us for the wrong we do. Anyway, don't you think we are all to blame for not taking better care of her? She was only a child you know, and after all none of us are perfect."

I did not remind him of it, but I happened to know of a homosexual affair he himself had not very long before this. However, I'm sure he would not have thought of it as being of equal evil importance, and at least not as bad in consequence.

While there was no fight, Antonio was confronted with what he had done. Now Jose and he were dissolving partnership as farmers. They divided the land the government had given them to work. But it was not as easy to divide up three burros. Finally, after many weeks of dispute, the judge decided that Jose should have the two younger ones and Antonio the older mother burro who was expecting another. This part is told in more detail in the book *Jewels of Mexico*.

Juana was now too ashamed to sit out on the doorstep embroidering blouses. She had become more sick and nervous because of the whole thing, and to defend herself was spreading an ugly lie.

One day when I was across town treating the sick, a woman said, "What a disgrace that a girl should have a baby by her own brother. Is that the kind of Christians you have?"

"What? Who do you mean?" I asked puzzled.

"Ah, you know, Maria. Juana was here and told me not to tell anybody, but that the real father of the child is Maria's own brother, Mauro."

"Well now, just a minute," I protested, "Or just wait a few months until you see that baby here in the market. He has the identical face of his father Antonio, Juana's brother. You'll see for yourself."

"For lands sake! I wonder why Juana goes around spreading such lies . . . but of course . . . she is defending her brother Antonio. How foolish of me not to see through that," she apologized. "Anyway, it is better that it was not the poor child's own brother," she added.

That Juana! She was more clever, really, than I expected. Soon she came up with a scheme which was a solution to the whole problem for the family, if not the best one for Maria.

Her older brother's wife had died just a few months before, leaving him with about six little ones. He was a drunkard who never came to church, always cursing us, everywhere he went. Juana took her troubles to him. Now he came forward nobly offering, "Since my brother is not in a position to take care of his responsibilities to this girl and his child, I will take her to wife and give her and the child a home."

About a year later I had the opportunity to visit Maria in her new home. She was grinding corn for a large family, and was again big with child.

Seemed to me she was getting enough punishment, or was it just the natural consequences of her misfortune and the way of life in Maria's small world.

CHAPTER

7

With summer came the rains, storms and mud. What mud! It sure was good to have a horse to get around to visit my patients, even there in town.

One night we were awakened by a terrific storm, thunder and lightning, sheets of rain and rushing water. Above it all, we could hear screaming and shouting from the people in the flat on the other side. Jumping up and looking out the window, I could see by flashes of lightning that our contented, gurgling creek had become an angry turbulent river. Lanterns and flashlights moved to and fro, as men were rescuing women and children from their humble homes.

Then all at once I noticed that my feet were getting wet. By my flashlight I saw water swirling out of Lola's room, and around the trunk which held my linens and clothing. She was also awake, and between us, we lifted the trunk up on chairs. By this time, we were ankle deep in water and continued to rescue the rest of the things on the floor. Then we discovered where the trouble was coming from. The mud wall built against the cliff was dissolving by the water running over and down the embankment. The brethren had forgotten to put a trench there. So, after putting on wraps, we grabbed a pick and a hoe and went out in the downpour to make a trench so that the water could run away from the house.

At the time, Lola had laryngitis and I was having my first symptoms of malaria. It was daybreak before we got the water and mud out of the house, but we felt fortunate, for some people didn't have a house anymore. It wouldn't be much of a problem to have someone plaster the wall with mud again. But we were isolated; it was several days before we could cross the creek, even on a horse. The foot bridge had been swept away. There was no market, no milk, nor even clear drinking water since the spring on the edge of the creek was under water. Nor were there communications with the outside world, for the roads were impassable.

On my sick visits through the village, Doña Mela, the sister of Don Julio, often came out of her little store on the plaza to invite me in for a soda-pop. Her sister, Lyla, who had come with La Chata to welcome me, lived nearby and was usually there. Then one day they sent for me to come to treat Doña Mela, who was sick. She had a high fever because of a terrible looking and badly swollen abscess. The only way she could be comfortable was lying on her face or on her side. She and her family believed that she had become infected because she had been given an injection by a pregnant woman. They explained that if they had known this, they wouldn't have gone to her. The irony of it was that the boyfriend who was to blame for the condition was her own son. Nor did he intend to marry the girl, for he said that he hadn't found her to be a "Señorita," that is a virgin, so according to their standards, that relieved him of all responsibility.

It took quite a while before the infection was under control well enough for them to treat it themselves. And since she was in bed, their elderly mother, Doña Loida, often came to visit, hobbling over the cobblestone square with a cane. She was a very interesting old lady and we soon became good friends. We had many discussions on Christianity, when I sometimes took the opportunity to quote Scriptures, like "The blood of Jesus Christ, cleanses us from all sin," and others which they accepted.

One day Don Julio said, "I can't imagine how you and my mother and sisters can be such good friends. How do you manage it? Don't you ever have religious discussions?"

"Oh, yes, but we stick to the essentials on which we agree, and when we get off on doctrines on which we don't, we respect each others' opinions, agreeing not to disagree."

"Well, now. It sure is surprising to hear that of them, but I guess anybody can change," he continued, twisting his moustache. "Anyway, I am going to give you one one bit of advice, my girl. They are awful gossips, so be careful what you say to them. Don't say anything you wouldn't want repeated, or stretched and changed here or there."

He was so right about the gossiping for I was learning all about everyone. One day when I came from the post office, where it appeared that Sr. Flores' wife looked sadder than usual, I mentioned to them that it seemed as though she had been crying.

They said, "Oh, yes, she is fretting because he has gone to town where he has another woman and family."

"How can that be?" I gulped with surprise. "Why he is so loving and devoted to his family here!"

"Oh yes, and he is just as devoted and loving to the others also," they commented smiling. "Anyway, don't feel too sorry for her. She brought it on herself. She knew he had this lovely blonde novia, sweetheart, that he intended to marry, but she wanted him, so she schemed and lied to separate them. And her brothers who were his pals, helped her by inviting him to stay nights with them when he was in town, which gave her a chance to make her advances. Then, when things went too far with them, her brothers threatened, 'Now you will marry our sister or else!' So he married her, but he still loved the other girl who forgave him and agreed to be his mistress. When he goes to town to spend a few days with her there, he takes her to the movies, and they stroll out evenings around the plaza with their children. There's no doubt she is still the one he loves best."

"Yes, and since his wife here is getting big with child, it is just natural that he will spend more time with the other one during this period," another person added. All of which left me somewhat stunned.

Using the sulfa drug helped very much with infections like Doña Mela had, and even more for pneumonia. After I used it on the first man who recovered, it became known as the miracle pill, and some people at least, were convinced that I had more power than the woman witch doctor of the village. In fact, Sulfadiazol was new in the States at this time. It had only come out while I was in nurse's training in Philadelphia, just prior to my coming to Mexico. Before using the sulfa, whenever one mentioned pneumonia to the people of this place, the family was ready to begin the death wail and prepare for the funeral. Now several had been saved, and people knew there were hopes. It also helped women with breast infections, babies with infected navels, and people who had been cut or shot.

And speaking of death wails, we were hearing them often at this time, especially at night. First there was an epidemic of measles, and there were at least two processions a day of little children being taken to the graveyard on the hill across from us. They called the little ones Angelitos, little angels, when they died. They were carried on a special bier with a canopy all decorated with lace and flowers, tinsel and crepe paper. The body was dressed like an angel, with a crown of flowers on its forehead. It was attended by four little girls, dressed in their confirmation dresses with crowns and veils, who walked before and behind the open coffin.

At the head of the processions marched the musicians playing different strains of classical music on their violins. One of the musical numbers was "The Glow Worm," which they played over and over. How strange to hear "The Glow Worm" and others played at a funeral procession. The idea was that it should not be a sad affair because the baby or young child was now a little angel, which I hoped was of some comfort to the poor bereaved mother and the family.

Sometimes they came to ask me if I had ribbons, lace or flowers to contribute, so I started to pick up such pretty things to have them on hand for these occasions.

Then there was an epidemic of typhoid. The carpenter's wife had it and she was expecting, but recovered. However, one of their little boys died, and the carpenter had malaria and needed injections. Malaria was very bad also, and I was injecting Don Julio and his son Luis, Sr. Flores, and many others including Don Segundo and his two teen-age boys. Since he was a widower, they had no woman to care for them; so they appreciated the teas and the broths I took to them and gave me bananas in exchange.

When Don Julio was better, Doña Dawn left for Mexico City to visit her beloved son, Marcos. There would be no school vacation until the first of December, for the schools closed in the winter instead of the summer, probably because there was no way of heating the school rooms. She took La Chata along and it was lonesome in downtown Chapulhuacanito. Don Julio appreciated it when I could stop for a chat and to share the news. We both agreed that the war propaganda on the radio was disgusting. Germany was making a big effort to get Mexico on her side, and the Fascists through the Sinarquists were now openly using the press, the radio and even the church.

Don Julio was on our side but sometimes he was almost convinced that they would win. And I was very concerned because my two youngest brothers, Bill and Eddie, were in the Army.

Then, too, there was the sad news of Christians still being martyred, especially in the state of Hidalgo, where some of Dr. Dale's Bible students came from. They told us of a self-appointed army Colonel who ruled their section with an iron hand.

Don Julio knew of him, the Colonel of Tehuacan, and said he was a wicked man who would not get away with the things he did if he were in our state of San Luis Potosi where we have liberty, law, and order.

But it took Don Julio's sisters to enlighten me in detail as to what some of those things were. Besides thinking it was his duty to kill Protestants, the Colonel felt he had the right to kill anyone he pleased. Also when a poor man was in bad straits from loss of crops or sickness, he would lend the man money. Then later if the unfortunate man could not pay, the big, husky brute would take his 13- or 14-year-old daughter whom he would rape and keep until she was pregnant or until he grew tired of her. Then he would send her home to her poor

64

parents again. Or, sometimes he would take the man's young son for payment and put him in his "army" without pay to become a more or less lawful bandit. Doña Mela lamented, "The worst part is that he claims to be a good Catholic, but he's a hypocrite who is a disgrace to us and to the Holy Virgin."

When Dr. Dale wrote that I was to get ready to leave for Mexico City to renew my passport and to attend the National Sunday School Convention there, I was happy for the opportunity to get away from the drudgery, heat and mud.

Sr. Flores and his wife became concerned when they heard that I was going to be away, so they decided that she should go to her mother in Tamazunchale to have her new baby. We arranged to go together. Sr. Flores said that way if anything happened along the trail, they would at least have a nurse with them.

He was very gentle and considerate of her all along the way, often getting down from his horse to guide hers by the reins through the mud and over the rougher spots. My esteem for him was restored to a great extent because of his concern.

CHAPTER

8

Being back in fascinating Mexico City was a needful and pleasant change, not only for me, but for Rev. Dale as well. He had been so sad and lonely since he lost his dear Katherine.

Stanley Jones was an inspiring speaker at the C.E. Convention we attended. We were encouraged by the fellowship of old friends.

When we returned to Tamazunchale, I stayed there over the weekend. That Sunday morning we received shocking news when the younger brothers of our best family in Laguna arrived pale and trembling. They came to tell us that their older brother and his daughter had been assassinated the night before.

It was the man who had brought his little boy to me after he had been bitten by a dog when I first arrived in Chapulhuacanito a few months before. He was such a nice person.

The story was that they were having a service in his home when a group of horsemen from San Felipe rode up encircling their humble home shouting, "Death to the Protestants." They started to shoot into the house where he was standing by the table in the lamplight, with an open Bible in his hands. When he was hit and started to slump, his fourteen year old daughter rushed up to her beloved father, throwing her arms around him, and one of the bullets hit her also. They fell together, clinging to each other in death. The others were fortunate to escape without harm, but were still being threatened.

Back in Chapulhuacanito, Lola had a lot of news to report. An Indian woman who had been in labor two or three days had died because she couldn't give birth. People said, "If you had been here Señorita, you might have saved her."

The woman's death had scared the Mayor's wife. Being afraid that I might not get back in time, she had gone to Tamazunchale to wait for her baby, as she had always done before.

Also, dear Doña Linda's pathetic little boy had died. She shed a few tears as she told me about it, but was comforted knowing that he was better off in the arms of Jesus.

Another bit of unexpected news was that the carpenter was in jail, and his wife expecting any day. He was suspected of having taken part in a robbery. That was sad, because he had come to church a few times and we had hoped that he would become a real Christian. Also, there was a personal reason for my being sorry about his being in jail. I was expecting him to put a ceiling in our house before cold weather came.

Therefore, it was indeed a relief for all concerned, when he was declared innocent in time to be home when the baby came.

They were anxious for me to help in the delivery, although she could have had it just as well without me. She would not lie down, and he said, "Let her do it the way she is used to having them." So, she squatted on her knees, pulling on the usual rope tied to the rafters. However, when the baby hit the floor, where I had newspapers placed so that it wouldn't fall in the dirt, she slumped back and let me take care of the placenta and the tying of the cord. They seemed to appreciate that I had lost the whole night's sleep to be there in case there was an unexpected difficulty.

Since they had suffered so much sickness and trouble, he asked me to lend them money in advance on the ceiling job; which he did later, and it was finished in time to keep us warmer when winter came.

One day about a week after returning home, our friend Professor Leo, came looking quite distraught. "What is wrong?" I asked, after the usual greetings.

"This," he replied, as he pulled an official looking letter from his shirt pocket. "They have sent me an order from headquarters in Pachuca, the capital of Hidalgo, to change schools."

"You mean in November, when the schools close, don't you?"

"No, right now!" he replied. "I have to report within two weeks to go to another rural school in an area even worse than this one, and I was so contented in my little village school here."

"Why, this is awful! You have done so well there, taking so much interest in the people; the educational department must have been misinformed. And the garden, tell me, has it produced anything yet?"

"Very little, but it will soon if they take care of it after I'm gone, which isn't likely. It will probably go to the chickens and the burros."

"Could this have happened because I had visited you there?"

"Who knows, but it seems unlikely that they would know about that in the Department of Education in the state capital."

We both agreed that there could be ways for them to find out. Perhaps one of the villagers, who went to the county seat, Huejutla beyond San Felipe, told the priest or some official when they went to market or confession over there. That would be enough for the complaint to travel.

"My wife wants us to go back to our own state of Queretaro, where there is religious liberty and a better culture. There we could live in safety, but I don't have the education to be a teacher in that state, and I can't work at hard labor."

That was evident, for this slim little man was not strong physically, and his problem was serious. Probably he was fortunate that he had not been shot as yet, or perhaps they were waiting to put the pressure on him at the new place. We never knew, for we never heard from him again.

Doña Dawn returned home, sooner than expected. She brought some new pictures of Marcos who was getting even better looking as he matured. She left La Chata in the city with him and hastened home because of her concern for her men folks.

Besides being concerned for their health and well-being, she always feared for their safety when they rode around the countryside.

When young Julio left with the soldiers his argument was that as long as those bandits were at large no one was safe; so if he could help capture them it would be for the good of the family and everybody. But of course they were not the only bandits around. How about our mailmen who were being robbed and killed? There was no doubt that it was not always the same gang.

Many times, at the end of a weary day, I would stop to rest at her house and she would be reluctant for me to leave, pleading, "Wait with me until the men get home." Then as she cleaned and polished the glass kerosene lamps, she would go to the door every now and then to listen, saying, "I wonder why it's taking them so long. It's getting dark. They know they shouldn't be out so late."

What a relief when the sound of horses' hoofs were heard and they came galloping across the cobblestones toward the house where we were waiting at the open door.

Now, I knew that Doña Dawn's interest in their retiring and moving to Tamazunchale was not purely for selfish reasons but for the safety of her loved ones. They were still living in the shadow of Don Pedro's murder on the trail.

Here in this primitive, out-of-the-way place the fear of death was indeed real. It stalked close to the poor and wealthy alike, in one way or another.

CHAPTER

9

Romance now hit our small circle. Andrea was going about in a trance, letting the beans burn and being very forgetful most of the time. I wondered who or what she was daydreaming about, until Lola told me that she was in love with Don Segundo's oldest son, Saturno. He seemed to be quite young to be serious, although the Indian boys and girls married very young.

Don Segundo himself was courting Andrea's older sister, Laura, in the Indian fashion. Every time he came to take care of the horse or came to church, he would hang around the door of their little hut, talking and laughing with the women inside, or sitting there with the mother. Laura was somewhat younger than he, but not really too much, and the poor man sure needed a wife.

About this time Rev. Dale sent us a new student preacher who came on the weekends. Julio Cuenca was a tall, nice-looking young man from beyond Pachuca, Hidalgo. He was a relative of our dear Doña Linda.

Each Saturday he brought us our mail, making that the "red-letter" day of the week. We had it brought from Tamazunchale because even my friend Sr. Flores at the Post Office had advised that it would be best to have our correspondence brought from town, because the mail out here was rather irregular and unsafe. In fact, just the short time I had been there, the mail, carried by pack mules and donkeys, had been robbed several times, and the mail carriers were usually killed. Sometimes it took a week or more to find someone brave enough to replace them.

Pastor Julio was Spanish-speaking, but he also knew Aztec well. Therefore, I asked him to teach me Aztec. So, each Saturday afternoon we would try to have a lesson, using the blackboard in the clinic. The list of words in my notebook grew into sentences to practice on my Indian patients, until before I left those parts I no longer needed Andrea to interpret for us.

While we were studying, Lola and Andrea were giggling more than usual out in the kitchen. And when Lola entered the room for something, Julio's attention would wander from the lesson, as his eyes followed her around.

Suddenly our timid Lolita had become so bashful, she could not even lift her eyes when she greeted Julio upon his arrival. It would have seemed that she didn't notice him at all, if one didn't know better. Finally, I rebuked her saying, "You are not very sociable to Julio. Can't you talk naturally to him, like you do to the boys at church?" She seemed almost conscience-striken, as she shook her head in the negative. Nor did she ever show any interest openly. However, we had reasons to believe she did in secret, for there were letters going back and forth at the village Post Office during the week. Poor fellow, no doubt as soon as he got back to school, he wrote what he didn't get a chance to say in person. And no doubt timid Lola could express herself better at a distance.

One morning, Andrea's little niece came to say that Andrea wasn't feeling well. What a surprise I got when later in the day I went over to the house to see her. She had a black eye and a swollen face.

"Do you know what happened to Andrea?" I asked Lola, when I got home.

"Yes, she and Laura had a fight down at the spring when they went to get water this morning. And that big ugly Laura beat her up."

"But why would she do that?"

"It's because of Saturno. She wants him instead of his father Don Segundo. And even though she knows that Andrea cares for him, Laura says she will get him nevertheless."

"Of all things! She is old enough to be his mother. Surely he wouldn't give up a lovely sweet young thing like Andrea for that skinny woman already showing her age, now would he?"

"I wouldn't be too sure, Señorita, for it seems that things have been going on between them for some time. And he is too young to really think for himself."

That night Laura disappeared. She and Saturno had gone off together. Now that it was no secret, I could console poor Andrea, who was heartbroken.

Don Segundo was in a much worse condition. His pride was hurt as much as his heart. He said he just couldn't face people around there anymore, especially Don Domingo Grande and his close friends, who sat on the stone fence talking and sneering about almost everybody, including my patients who came for medicines. They had been taunting him lately because of his helping me. "So you have a woman to boss you now," they jeered. "You must be getting rich with the money the Americana gives you. Does she pay you in pesos or dollars?" The fact was that the poor man was being paid very little.

They were also envious because he spoke better Spanish than anyone in the congregation, which instead of being appreciated was a barrier as far as they were concerned.

His plans were to go to Tamazunchale for a few days, and he confided that he was going to ask Rev. Dale for work as an evangelist, hoping that he would accept him and send him away as far as possible.

He said that his younger boy, Falvio, would be staying with a relative until his brother and new wife returned. Then he offered, "He can help you with your horse until you find someone else."

The someone was Pedro, a boy of about twelve. Rev. Dale sent him to me with Pastor Julio and a note, saying that the little boy had no mother and his father had come to study at the Bible School. They didn't know what to do with Pedro there, and knowing that I needed someone to help with the horse, they hoped that I would keep him.

Pedro seemed happy to be a part of our family. He was a nice boy who took good care of the horse, taking him to water and to pasture. He also took the horse to the forest to get wood, tying it in bundles to the horse's saddle. This was a big help, for it was difficult to get wood these days, for no one came around to sell lately.

The first ones who came I will never forget. One day a woman's voice came calling, "Wood for sale." There on the path outside the door were two Spanish-speaking women, mother and daughter, with a donkey loaded with wood. They looked gypsy-like with their long skirts tucked up in front in order to work and walk more freely.

The one who took my attention was the beautiful girl of about sixteen with a cluster of dark curls and rosy cheeks. She gave the impression that at any moment now she would throw up her arms in a graceful gesture, taking off in a Spanish tango or gypsy dance. Naturally, it was far beyond them to know anything about my imaginations. The mother was explaining in a doleful voice why they had to stoop to selling wood. "My husband died and all he left us was our little chosita, cabin, and this little donkey. So we have to put him to work to buy our daily bread."

We gladly paid her what she asked for the load of wood, and thereafter, she brought it every week. Until one week they didn't come. The beautiful girl Kathryn had eloped with one of the traveling merchants who came to market. That affair was to end very badly for that misled young girl.

The only romance coming to the natural happy end at the time, was that of Andrea's cousin, Carlotta, who lived nearby. She was to have a wedding in the church in the near future.

CHAPTER

10

Balmy Indian-summer days had come. The summer heat was over and rains were gone, the mud dried up, and the ripened corn rustled softly in the gentle breeze as the fields basked in the soft autumn sunshine.

There was excitement and mystery in the air, as everybody was getting ready for the Day of the Dead, or All Saints Day, which is taken seriously in Mexico.

The last week in October, we had an extra big market day. There were many candles, flowers, fireworks, paper decorations, tinsel, religious pictures, special candies and breads and extra fruit for sale.

The celebration which lasted for three days, had a little bit of our Decoration Day, Fourth of July, Halloween, Thanksgiving and Christmas all in one.

The homes in this area of Mexico were decorated with altars in one of the corners. Doña Dawn's was elegant, made with a big arch framework, covered with flowers and placed over a large table. There were tiers, or shelves, with candles, pictures, flowers, food and other pretty objects on them.

Some of the people took plates and baskets of food, and others took flowers to the graves of loved ones. And there were many brightly strewn paths made of the petals of marigolds, often called the flowers of the dead, leading from the Indian homes to the graveyard. These were to help the spirits of the departed to find their way back to their former homes where plates of food were waiting for them on the altar. Some of the relatives were in prayer before the lighted candles, while others were drinking themselves drunk.

The first morning of the fiesta, I was awakened by the sound of music, a serenade. What a surprise to see the serenaders at my gate, our few town musicians with Don Julio, Sr. Flores, Don Solamon, the Mayor and others. "We bring greetings to the living this morning," they said, "for we want you to know that we appreciate what you are doing for us and our people."

Then they invited me to their homes saying, "Our women folks want you to come over for breakfast." So, I made the rounds until I was so full of tamales, chocolate, corn cakes and other good things, that I just couldn't eat any more. All the while, Lola was collecting plates of food being sent to our house. Needless to say, Pedrito was in his glory, getting himself stuffed also.

Our preacher boy, Julio, arrived that afternoon, suggesting that I go on a trip to Lagunilla and Huejutla, the county seat, the next morning. "We can make it in a day, if we start early enough. Rev. Dale wants me to go, because some of the new believers there are relatives of mine. And he thinks you could help them also."

Knowing that we would have to go through San Felipe, where there was danger, I asked, "How is the government investigation of the killing of the Indian brother and his daughter coming along?"

"Oh, the government sent some representatives to

reprehend the officials of San Felipe for what had happened. And you know what the Mayor there told them, he said, 'Tell the President to run his business in Mexico City, I'm running mine here in San Felipe.' "

"Would you be using a horse this time?" I asked hopefully.

"No, you can, but I would not want to offend the poor brethren who don't have any. And another student is going along with us on foot."

All things considered, I was rather reluctant about going; yet I did want to see those places, so we prepared to leave. Being busy, I did not prepare lunch, thinking we could buy something in San Felipe. But when we arrived in that small town, most of the stores were closed, and the ones that were open had nothing on the shelves. Everything had been taken to the graveyard as offerings. Pastor Julio remarked dolefully, "One has to be dead to get anything to eat today."

Finally, as we were leaving town, we found one little store with a few items. The woman was very inquisitive, asking many questions, like, "Where are you coming from? Where are you going? When are you coming back?"

Being very naive, I answered, "Friday."

After we left, Julio rebuked me for telling her all I knew. "They may lie in wait for us Friday," he pointed out. "Now we will have to cut our trip short, coming back Thursday. You know they have warned us that no preachers will be able to pass through here alive." He looked back over his shoulder for quite some distance, with a worried look on his face.

Again, I wished that they, too, were riding horses, so we could get away from that place faster. However, it was evident that the people of San Felipe were more interested in the dead than in the living that day.

The trip was quite uneventful, as we climbed mountains and forded rivers, until we came upon a huge cobra snake, coiled on the narrow path. Other travelers were arriving on the other side of the snake and all traffic was stopped. My horse was so restless because of the snake that I decided to get down. When enough men had gathered on both sides, they picked up stones and decided to attack the stubborn reptile. At the first stone, it drew itself up angrily, blowing it's head up to the size of a cat's head. The stones were well aimed and it was soon dead. I threw a few, too, but doubt that mine had any effect.

We took the dead snake along to Lagunilla, where a man dressed the skin, which was about eight feet long. I kept it as a trophy of the trip.

Pastor Julio had a married cousin there. He, Ramon, was a tall lanky, rough-looking fellow, who had just recently become a Christian and who was receiving much opposition. He and his family had come down from the mountains of Hidalgo because of the persecution there, and they wanted to move to our little village of Chapulhuacanito.

Ramon was working for a well-to-do ranch owner, who lived in a large hacienda which had seen better days. However, even now, after the Revolution, he and his sons still thought they should run the countryside. He was one of the many "Caciques," local rulers, of Mexico. They wanted to meet the American girl, probably because I was the first to come their way. So, Ramon took me to visit and we were received royally. One good-looking young son who was studying in Mexico City practiced his English with me, and the refined, jovial, old gentleman talked religion very intelligently.

As we came down the hill from the long, low, Mexican

house with its courtyards, we crossed the bridge of a small creek, where a dead horse lay on the bank below. It smelled awful! After getting far enough away to take my hand from my nose and mouth, I asked Ramon why the horse died.

"One of the ranch owner's sons shot it in a fit of drunken temper," he replied. "Even people don't escape their kind. That's why I want to move away while I'm still alive," he added.

How sad, I mused to myself, and they seemed so cultured and nice on the surface.

The next morning, I saw one of the most beautiful sights I have ever seen in Mexico. The people were taking their babies, small animals, fruit and garden products to be presented and blessed at the picturesque chapel on a high knoll overlooking the village. A priest had come for this special day. The arched gate and the church were decorated with flowers and streamers. Even the pathway leading to it was strewn with many marigold petals. There was a long, winding procession of people in colorful fiesta dress, with baskets of food and flowers on their heads, leading little ones by the hand and with babies slinging in shawls on their backs; while here and there among them, a lamb, calf, or other small animal was being led or carried.

"Oh, how beautiful!" I exclaimed. "I must get my camera."

"Indeed not!" Julio protested firmly. "The head man of this village has said that if you are so much as seen carrying a camera they will put you in jail. And that little windowless hut is not a pleasant place to be." The house we stayed in had plenty of insects, and I knew the jail would surely be worse. So I had to forfeit a very pretty picture.

That day we went to nearby Huehutla, the fanatical county seat. We stopped to visit a school teacher who was favorably impressed with the Gospel, but felt he couldn't let it be known. His family all looked very nervous at our presence, so we cut the visit short. Remembering about my other teacher friend, I knew they had good reasons.

Huehutla was at the base of the mountain which I could see from my patio, thirty miles away. The mountain was beautiful, but the place was disappointing. The people were not friendly-looking. After seeing the plaza, which was not pretty as were most of the typical green, lovely park-like plazas of Mexico; we started back to Lagunilla where we had more work to do, Pastor Julio to preach and me to treat the sick.

When it was time to leave, the brethren told Julio of a path on the other side of the mountain which did not go through San Felipe. Although it was longer and very rough it was safer, so we decided to go that way.

Ramon's niece, Aurelia, a very sweet teenage orphan girl, wanted to come back with us. I was very glad to bring her, for we needed someone to take Andrea's place. Poor Andrea, since her sister left, she had to do all the housework at home, bringing water from the spring, washing clothes and everything. So, she no longer had time to come in to help us.

Ramon found a horse for Aurelia to ride and he came along with us, in order to take it back. Also he wanted to see our brethren about getting some of the government "Ejido," or communal land, which was being given to the poor and which he was able to get later on.

Finally at dusk, we were in sight of Chapulhuacanito, saddleworn, exhausted and weak from having eaten very little all day. The prospect of a refreshing bath was urging me on, being full of ticks and insect bites. But as we entered town, we were stopped by a man who came running to meet us. He was the young husband of a girl expecting her first baby.

"Oh, Señorita, at last you have come! My wife has been in pain for two days. We had almost given up hope of your arriving before she dies."

Immediately, I sent for my obstetrical bag which had everything in it sterilized, including the obstetrical instrument forceps. After doing all I could, we could see it was impossible for the child to be born without extra help, so reluctantly and prayerfully I used the forceps to help pull out the baby's head.

He was born blue and limp and I worked desperately for the next twenty minutes, shaking and spanking him, using hot and cold water baths, and finally giving artificial respiration before he gave his first gasp for breath.

By the time I staggered into my house with shaking knees, I slumped into bed without the bath. But how thankful I was to have arrived in time to save that woman and her child, by God's help.

It was a good thing that we returned a day earlier than pastor Julio had originally planned. Our God and Guide makes all things work together for good as I had seen all through the trip.

CHAPTER

11

The tall, graceful young man on Don Julio's white horse presented a striking figure as he rode forth from the Hervert's courtyard in the direction of the sugar cane ranch. When he saw me crossing the cobblestone plaza with my medical bag, he smoothly swung the horse around in cowboy fashion, and came galloping casually toward me.

"You must be Mae," he greeted, as he reined in his spirited horse and leaned over the saddle. "My folks have told me all about you."

"And you must be Marcos. We've been waiting for you, and I'm glad you are home."

"So am I. It will be good to help my Dad on the ranch for awhile. I hope you will be at our house when we return in the afternoon." Then, with an enchanting smile, he was off, riding with graceful dignity. But just before he was out of sight, he turned to wave.

Later on, he told me of his impression of our first meeting saying, "You appeared like an angel of mercy in your white uniform as you skipped across those cobblestones in the early morning mist."

La Chata was preparing for a family picnic at San Pedro, the sugar ranch, where they had a mill for making brown sugar, called "pilon." They invited me to go along.

The ranch with the mill was not strange to me, for we always passed it on the way to the village of "Frijolia" (Free-hoe-leah, meaning little bean), where we had a church and where I frequently went to teach, and to treat the sick. We often stopped at San Pedro, where Don Julio had a settlement of mud houses for the manager, cook, and other plantation workers and their families, who sometimes needed medical treatment.

The ride out that way was always pleasant, for it led along the creek with its shady paths and overhanging trees, then through a field of tall, graceful bamboo which intertwined overhead. However, today it was an especially enjoyable ride, with a festive spirit added, since we were celebrating Marcos' return home. Even Doña Dawn had been persuaded to come along. She didn't seem to mind when Marcos and I gleefully raced our horses up the wider slopes where we waited for her to catch up, as she was riding side-saddle.

When we arrived, La Chata and her mother went to the kitchen to prepare the dinner. Being a rather cool winter day, Marcos and I sat near the big oven in the mill, where we became better acquainted, while shelling peanuts and nuts which La Chata wanted to put into the brown sugar syrup to make a tasty candy. After awhile, she came to tell us that dinner was ready and we gathered at the table with their brother Luis and Don Julio.

The mill was fascinating. Patient horses and mules driven in circles churned out the juice of the sugar cane which flowed through an old fashioned wooden channel into large steel tubs. The tubs were placed on grates heated by fires on a lower level. When the syrup was boiled to a certain point, it was poured into clay molds shaped like cones. When cooled it was removed and the pilon, or brown sugar, was now ready for use.

Another use for the sugar cane was to make native rum which they called aguardiente.* Don Julio and some of his neighbors made the rum in something like a big still, only here it wasn't unlawful. They never spoke of the place and I never saw it, but I knew one of his nephews was the manager.

The sugar cane fields themselves, were like a magnificent green, moving sea, waving in the breeze, as far as the eye could see along the fertile river valley.

The war news was sad and fearful these days. My brother, Bill, was expecting to be sent to Germany any day and Eddie was stationed in Hawaii. Also there were other friends and relatives involved.

December 7th, Don Julio and I were sitting by the radio. La Chata and Marcos had gone to town. Doña Dawn was putting supper on the table, when shocking news flashed across the air with terrific impact, "Pearl Harbor was bombed by the Japanese at 4 a.m. this morning. Thousands are dead and many more missing. More details later."

My stunned mind repeated the words, "Pearl Harbor — Hawaii — thousands dead and missing — Eddie, my baby brother, was he one of them? Oh, no!" With this I put my head down on the table on my arms and sobbed.

Loving, tender, fatherly and motherly hands stroked my hair and patted my shoulder. "Don't cry. Your brother is probably all right. Perhaps he wasn't at that place. Dios es Grande!"

Later on, more news broadcasts gave us the details. The Navy men were the ones hit, not so much the Army. In a few

*See Glossary, pages 173-174

weeks a letter from home assured me that Eddie was all right. He was a Sergeant stationed at Schoffield Barracks nearby where they did have about 150 casualties. However, his plans were now changed. He had completed his army term and was waiting for discharge; but was now called to more active duty instead. Later he was sent to Germany where Bill was sent also. Both were in the worst of the fighting, yet God kept them from even being wounded. Yes, God is Great!

One thing the bombing of Pearl Harbor did was to put Mexico more strongly on the side of the States. Before that, many listened to the Spanish and Italian Fascist propaganda because they were more or less Latin relatives. Even Germany had always been greatly admired because of their advancement in science and industry. Many Mexicans appreciated the German immigrants because of their honesty and diligence. But as for the Japanese, the Mexicans couldn't relate to them! The atrocity in the bombing of Pearl Harbor had made them aware of the danger involved, perhaps even to themselves.

This year, 1941, was to be a sad Christmas season for most of the world. But the world and its wars was far removed from Indian land. Here, our churches were preparing their Christmas programs. It was their one big fiesta of the year. Lola was practicing with the children and young people here and in Huichilingo (Wee-chil- lingo), a village only a few miles away but across the state line of Hidalgo.

The first time I rode over there was on a beautiful, moonlight night when I went to treat a believer with a very severe attack of malaria.

One of the things that always impressed me about their village was the steeple of the big Catholic Church. It sat in front of the church instead of on the top of it, looking as though it had slid down and settled there. However, it was built that way so that the bell could be rung easier by the sexton. Later I was to see other churches in this area built in like manner.

The believers there had such a nice humble friendly spirit. There was Juan and his five married brothers, the carpenter Jose, a fatherly Indian man, who was the leader of the congregation and sweet little Maria, who had been in the Doctora's school for Indian girls. Maria's story "The Long Black Box" is in the book *Jewels of Mexico.*

Our Indians went in merry-making groups, visiting each other's Christmas programs, being welcomed heartily and treated to tamales wherever they went. My house was full of visitors for about a week. This year we had a lovely season. The weather was perfect.

At Chapulhuacanito we had a packed church with people standing outside. Don Julio, Marcos, and Luis were there, sitting on the front seats. Also Sr. Flores and other people from the center of town. The church was decorated with beautiful hanging vines suspended from the rafters and with huge poinsettias. The setting was beautiful.

The Indians' coloring and features gave a naturalness to the parts they played of Bible characters in the Christmas Story. In one of the dramas, I took the part of a nurse. It was the same part I had been given when I was in Tamazunchale the year before. And of course, I played the Christmas carols on the little organ, while the congregation sang them beautifully. Many people went home marveling that Indians could perform as well as they did.

About twenty women and girls went along with the men to the program at Huichilingo. The carpenter cleaned out his shop to give us women a place to sleep on the floor there after the Christmas service. Perhaps some slept, but I couldn't. We were packed in so close that I was afraid to move for fear of getting my feet in the hair of the women sleeping at my foot-end and the feet of the girl at my head-end were too close to my face for comfort. Besides, who could lie without moving with all those fleas jumping around on us.

It was late, for the program had been long. However, I could still hear the familiar pat-pat of the women making tortillas. So, I got up and went to the kitchen where they were preparing the food for the next day. The carpenter had a nice fire on the dirt floor, where they were cooking the tamales. It was cold, so I sat by the fire with him until the wee hours. The women finished their work about midnight and had laid down there to sleep, while he kept the fire going. Every now and then, he would quote Scripture verses over and over again, probably to keep awake. The most frequent one was, "Be ye faithful unto death, and I will give you a crown of life," a verse which he no doubt had repeated other nights when he was in jail because of his love and faithfulness to Christ.

Before dawn, I, too, laid down beside the women near the fire for a few hours sleep.

This year we were celebrating Christmas here in peace, but next year was to be a different story.

CHAPTER

12

Kathryn, our gypsy-looking girl, was back, sick and heartbroken. The man had deserted her. The people where she had stayed had given her the bus fare to get home.

Her mother explained that when she eloped with him, he took her to a witch doctor who lived in a cave in the hills somewhere toward Tampico. That old medicine man acted as sort of a priest as well. He performed some sort of a spiritual marriage ceremony for them. I thought to myself, "Big deal, soothing the woman's conscience while giving the man no responsiblity on his part." The man continued to go around as a traveling salesman in the villages at their weekly markets, leaving her with relatives until after awhile he didn't come back.

After examining her thoroughly, it was evident that she had had an abortion and still had a bad infection. She was in a semi-coma with a high fever and no desire to live. She wouldn't taste anything her mother tried to give her.

The first thing that we did was to assure her that her mother loved her very much and was glad to have her only child back home again.

The sulfa pills were sufficient to take care of the infection, together with the treatments applied every day. I didn't mind going to see her daily on my sick rounds, for she needed all the friendship and spiritual help it was possible to give her. After she accepted Christ as her personal Savior and was rid of her guilt complex, she had a new purpose to live and picked up fast, coming back to a semblance of her former self. She started going along to the creek with her mother to bathe and wash clothes and to the woods to hunt sticks for their fire. The mother had sold the burro long ago in order to exist.

Kathryn now came to Sunday School and stayed to dinner with us each Sunday. But our Indian brethren would not accept her. Perhaps they were afraid that one of their young men would become interested in this "fallen woman."

Later on, she got housework in Tamazunchale and found someone who appreciated her. It was a common-law marriage but one that was permanent. For a girl in her situation that was as much as could be expected.

It was at their house during Kathryn's illness that I met the witch doctor, for she was the mother's sister. One day when Kathryn was getting well, I saw a pan full of strange objects soaking in water; a tiny metal cross, a sea shell, a bone and other objects, mostly stones.

"What is this?" I asked her mother.

"Oh, that is holy water," she answered. My sister is making it for Kathryn to help her get well."

"Why didn't you treat her with this instead of coming to me when she was so sick she almost died?" thinking to myself that probably this "holy water" would now get all the credit for what I had done.

"Oh, my sister had the holy objects in another village where she was treating a sick family," she explained.

"What kind of sickness did they have?"

"They had measles, and one of the children died of a bad cough that set in."

"Did you boil this stuff you brewed?" I asked, thinking of these objects being dragged around from one infected family to another.

About that time the curandera herself arrived. After greetings, we continued the discussion about the boiling of the objects. Knowing that I couldn't stop her from using them, I thought it would at least be helpful if I could possibly improve on the treatment. "I have been telling your sister that it would be better if you boiled these holy objects," I ventured to suggest. "Sick people shouldn't drink unboiled water, you know."

"Yes, that's right; they shouldn't drink raw water," they agreed. "But the objects might wear out sooner if they are boiled."

"Well, then, why not boil the water, and when it is still boiling, pour it over the things."

"Yes, that's a good idea," they agreed.

Being curious, I asked her to explain the things to me. "Where did they come from?" I asked.

The cross had been blessed by a certain important priest, and one of the stones was from the hillside at the shrine of the Virgin of Guadalupe near Mexico City. Another stone was from a spring where the "image of a saint" was found, which is kept in a church in Tesotla, a village in the mountains near us.

The connection was familiar to me, for that "stone saint" which was found in a brook had a slight resemblance to an idol which was supposed to have miraculous healing powers. The superstitious sick of our village prayed to it and made vows that if or when they got well, they would make a pilgrimage to the church at Tesotla and take an offering to the saint.

Once a year they brought this crude stone idol to our

town in a glass box, parading it around to the tune of instruments playing festive music.

There was another strange looking stone; so I finished by asking her where that was from.

"Oh, that is from a cave over at Huilitla (wee-leet-la), where a holy man does miracles."

"You mean the same 'holy man' who performed the spiritual marriage for Kathryn?"

They were rather embarrassed as they had to admit that it was the same one.

The curandera herself became one of my patients. She had pneumonia and was sure she was going to die. So, she sent for me. What a fear of death she had!

"Now if you feel you are going to die," I counseled, "the thing to do is to get prepared." So, I explained the way of salvation through Christ to her, reading the Bible and praying with her.

The next day when I arrived, she was a different person. Everything was all right. She was happy because she was going to get well. She had a wonderful experience the night before, when she was praying to the Lord, as I had told her to. She said He came and stood by her bedside and told her to follow Him. Now, she vowed that she was going to serve Christ and join our church on the hill. I was elated to think that we were to have a converted witch doctor.

Up to that time, her Catholic relatives and neighbors had not bothered about her. Now, all of a sudden, they realized that they had neglected her and that she was getting too much Protestant influence. After that, she was never alone when I went to see her. One could tell that they were building up a wall of protection around her. Also they were bringing her broths and things to eat, giving her all kinds of attention which they never gave before.

She didn't follow through about coming to our church, but she did stop beating her boys for coming to Sunday School. She also apologized about not coming herself, saying she would like to but she couldn't give up her profession nor her church, for she had to consider her means of making a living.

However, she remained one of my most regular patients often buying medicines for her followers. She tried to show me her appreciation and friendship by giving me a lovely little square doily of exquisite drawn work, which she took off the shelf where she had kept the image of the virgin. The little doily, which I have always prized, is about worn out.

CHAPTER

13

The flower garden in my tiny patio was beautiful that next spring. It was now a year since I had come here to live. Many of my friends came to sit for awhile on the low stone wall which we had built at the precipice overlooking the town and the mountains beyond.

There were tall poinsettias with huge flowers, which had given cheer all winter. They were planted beside the tall bamboo fence. Roses were blooming in the center flower bed, and morning glories climbed over the fence by the blue gate that led up to the toilet, just as I had planned. There was a bench below our bedroom windows under the eaves of the thatched roof.

Puttering in the garden was my recreation, when problems overwhelmed and nerves were tattered. It was also good therapy for my patients to sit on the bench while telling me about their ailments and troubles.

All the family had a part in the little garden. Aurelia faithfully saved all the bath water for the plants. And Pedro went to the creek for extra water when most needed.

It was really an oasis in the dire surroundings of our desolate-looking compound, where the patios were more like barnyards.

La Chata was one of my most frequent visitors, bringing others with her. Naturally, she brought Marcos when he was home, for he wanted to see the house and garden where their friend Mae lived.

Nowadays when Doña Dawn wanted to share a letter with me from him, she found a more willing and interested listener. When he first returned to the city, he had written a lovely letter to me. However, we were not corresponding for, being very busy, I was content for the time being to be mentioned at the end of his letter among the people she was to give his "saludos," greetings, to. Usually his grandmother and I were on the list.

Among the unusual cases mentioned in my diary were a few with all the symptoms of black-water fever. Upon conferring with the county health doctor in town, he said that there were other cases around there at the time, and as usual he gave the needed medicines and helpful instructions.

Another almost unbelievable case was that of a man who seemed to have acute appendicitis. At least that's where the trouble was located. He had a high fever and was in agony. I gave him sulfa pills and put compresses of anticongestive salve on the area. The abcess, with very little help from my knife, burst to the outside, and what a mess! After draining for some time, it closed and the man got well. That's something I could never prove nor explain apart from God's healing power.

Little Pedro was not well. He dragged around, hardly able to take the horse to water and pasture, much less to get wood. The tonic I had given him and the malaria treatment didn't seem to help. Aurelia, who mothered him, saw that he took his medicine, so we knew it wasn't that. We strongly suspected that it was because he was sleeping with the gang in the banana grove in front of our house, and that the older boys were draining him of his vitality.

When Pedro first came to us, we arranged for him to sleep at Doña Linda's house, because we had been warned that sex perversion was very common among the Indians and because our house was just too small for a twelve-year-old boy to stay there at night. We didn't even have doors on our partitions, just curtains. Then, after awhile, we were surprised to learn that he wasn't staying at Doña Linda's any more. When we asked him about it, he said that the gang had obligated him to come sleep with them, threatening to lie in wait and beat him up if he didn't.

When Pastor Julio came and we talked over the problem with him, he consoled us by saying, "Don't worry; Pedro has a grandmother and aunts to care for him if he is not well. I will take him to town with me, and next weekend his father can take him to their village."

There was one other problem we wanted to solve about Pedro. Aurelia, who took care of our change box in the clinic, was worried that money had been missing. Andrea told her that she overheard her brothers talking about Pedro giving them money. When we asked him about it, he admitted that it was true, saying that they had made him bring them the money, or else! Poor Pedro, he had been having a rough time without us suspecting it. In fact, he was going through the same trials, temptations and dangers that a boy his age would go through in the worst sections of a big city.

We missed Pedro, but we didn't really need him much. The horse could always be pastured with those of Don Julio. And we didn't need much wood any more, because we had now modernized our kitchen with a two-burner kerosene stove. We even had a little tin oven to put on it for baking. That was a novelty and our Indian friends came to see it with wonder. It was quite a luxury, for now we could have baked potatoes, salmon loaf and even birthday cakes.

Nor was I well, and that was putting it mildly. We were having an epidemic of dysentery and I had it, badly, with all the signs and pains of it being Amoebic. The doctor in Tamazunchale treated me, but Rev. Dale thought I should go to the hospital in Puebla for tests. It was also time for my passport to be renewed; so he advised, "Go get things in shape out there in the village in order to be away a month, so that you can get well."

On my way back from town that time, Don Miguel went with me again. It seemed like a long time since that first day when he helped me move out to the village. The summer rains had come, and it was muddy. The creeks were swollen and it was raining, so we rode with Mexican rain capes made of rubber, which were hot and heavy.

The mud made traveling slow, and in the afternoon when we came to the half-way point, the stream was a turbulent torrent. There must have been a cloudburst somewhere upstream.

Would my little horse be strong enough to withstand that current? I wondered, looking down to the left where the angry water splashed with a thunderous roar to the precipice far below. But, Don Miguel didn't give me much time to hesitate. He was looking upstream.

"Hurry," he yelled above the noise of the water. "My bigger horse will take the force of the current. Just stay close to me. Vamanos!" Let's go.

In seconds we were in and across. Then, just as we arrived safely up on the opposite bank, there was an ear-splitting noise, and looking back we saw a wall of water with tree trunks and boulders rushing down to the depths below.

"Gracias a Dios, we made it!" exclaimed Don Miguel. "I saw that upstream there was a dam being held back by some weak young trees, and I knew that if we didn't get across before it broke, we would be stranded out here in the forest in the rain for hours."

Yes, and in the dark without shelter, I thought with a grateful heart that we were on the homeward side.

CHAPTER

14

Puebla is a delightfully cool city, setting up near the snow-capped volcanoes. The supervisors and doctors of the hospital were friendly Americans, and the little Mexican girls in training were so sweet. One of the doctors said I had enough different kinds of animals in me to start a circus. Fortunately there was nothing incurable, and I did not need to be a bed patient at that time.

The doctor prescribed the treatment and allowed me to go wherever I wished saying he wanted to see me in ten days.

A few days were spent in lovely Cuernavaca with the Presleys, Presbyterian missionaries. Years later, after a severe heart attack, I would be living in that delightful city of "Eternal Spring," with its profusion of flowers all year round.

From there I went to Mitlan, Oaxaca, to the translation center of my Wycliffe friends to visit the Leals and Millers. Wandering around the ancient pre-conquest Indian ruins was a special pleasure. Also, it was very interesting to visit the shops and watch them weave their famous blankets and tablecloths of which I bought samples.

Back in Puebla, there were more tests and injections to be taken. In spite of that, the remaining days were pleasant. The Methodist Church had a bazaar where they sold ice cream and waffles. And the Baptist Church had a baptismal service one Sunday. The organ music, choir and message were all refreshing to one who had been away from it all for so long.

The next two weeks were spent in Mexico City. Each morning I went to the Immigration Office to renew my passport, and each day they would say "mañana", tomorrow.

The afternoons were usually spent visiting friends including the Hervert family, who were also in the city at that time.

Before we had left Chapulhuacanito, they urged me to visit them. La Chata said, "You must come to see us in the city. Marcos is expecting you. He will take us to Chapultepec castle and park, and Xochimilco and all around the city."

They were staying with an aunt, a sister-in-law of Doña Dawn, who had two single daughters. The sad part was that one of the girls, Tina, was in bed, dying of tuberculosis She was an exquisitely beautiful girl, even in her wasted-away condition.

"You can talk to Tina about her soul," suggested Marcos. "Don't you have some of those little papers you always carry? She likes to read." It was sometimes difficult to tell how serious he was, with that twinkle in his eyes. It was easy to talk and pray with her, for she was looking for peace and assurance. Therefore, she accepted readily and was comforted.

Ricardo, a close friend of Marcos had come to the city also. He was a musician and a clown. They often sat at the foot-end of her bed and sang popular songs to cheer her. No one seemed to be afraid of her contagious disease.

Ricardo was a tall, blond young man from San Martin, a town some twenty miles from Tamazunchale, which had been founded by the French and Spanish. They had kept pretty much to themselves so most of them were light-complexioned, and some were really blondes.

Marcos was in school in the mornings, but Ricardo wasn't. He said he was in the city looking for work. The kind of work he wanted was to be a radio singer, which perhaps he could have been with the right promotion and backing. Later, he settled for being a State trooper. For the time being, he was a playboy and kept Marcos from his studies when he visited, as Doña Dawn complained.

One afternoon, he and Marcos, La Chata and I went to historical Chapultepec, visiting the castle, the zoo and then enjoying a canoe ride on the lake. One thing which seemed strange to me was that Marcos was always careful to keep La Chata close to me, not letting her pair off with Ricardo.

"Why don't you want Ricardo to walk or sit with La Chata?" I asked. "Aren't you real good friends?"

"Oh, yes, he's all right as a companion for me, but my family wouldn't want him to get any ideas about marrying my sister," he replied.

Perhaps that is to be understood, I thought, since they are considered of the upper class in their part of the country.

One day Marcos asked me to meet him at the fountain beside the big cathedral on the Zocalo, city square. His dear old grandmother, Doña Eloida, was in the city also, staying with other relatives. She had come for the last time, especially to visit her beloved cathedral. That day Marcos had taken her there early in the morning before going to school. Then, he was to go back for her after lunch. That's when we met and sat "encantados" (enchanted) at the fountain awhile before going into the beautiful, impressive old cathedral for her. However, she wasn't ready to go.

"Just wait a little," she begged, as she continued to say her rosary. We knelt until our knees got tired, then sat until we got tired, then went out to the fountain in the sunlight, where the pigeons soared overhead and the music of the water added to the romantic atmosphere.

"My grandmother has been here all day and still doesn't want to leave, " Marcos contemplated. "She is so taken up with her communicating with God. I know you enjoy your religion, Mae, and I like it, the reasonableness of it. But you see my grandmother certainly gets something out of hers also, or she wouldn't be here all day in fasting and prayer." It certainly couldn't be denied.

Finally, Marcos went in and brought her out, saying, "Come now, Grandma, I have to take you home, then take Mae to where she stays in Coyoacan. They are expecting her there for dinner tonight. Then, I have to prepare my lessons for tomorrow morning." So she was persuaded to go, with the hope of coming back the next day.

On Sunday, there was a family picnic at intriguing, beautiful Xochilmilco, the Floating Gardens. We met at the Zocalo again and took a trolley to the park, consisting of waterways, Mexico's Venice. These are the last of the waterways, which at one time covered the site of Mexico City when it was the Aztec capital and its people went up and down the streets in canoes.

Marcos rented a float decorated with flowers, which was big enough for all the cousins and friends of the party. Our lunch boxes were put on a table in the center. Other boat floats went by with laughing, happy people. Many of them were on their honeymoon. Some boats had musicians called Mariachis, with their marimbas and other instruments, playing the old favorites, "Las Golondrinas", "La Paloma", "Barcos de Oro" and also popular music of the day. Ricardo and Marcos sang a few lovely duets to the music.

There were also canoes paddled by the descendants of their once proud Aztec race, who sold tacos and soda pops. The most picturesque were the women with their little canoes full of flowers. Marcos bought me gardenias and violets. In fact, I was the honored guest that day. Xochimilco is still an intriguing place to me even though I have been there several times since that day.

Within a few days my passport was renewed, and it was time to say "goodbye" to my attentive friends and prepare to return to my work. There was still a little last-minute shopping to do and medicines to be ordered and sent from a German Medical Supply house. I wound up these things as fast as possible, for I was now anxious to get home and learn how everything was back there in the village.

CHAPTER

15

Upon returning to Chapulhaucanito, the biggest news awaiting me was that Pastor Julio had been changed to another church, and we now had a new student pastor.

That Pastor Julio and Lola were now novios was an established fact. Most missions don't like to have sweethearts together with a long courtship existing, so they felt it wise to change him when I went on vacation. Poor Lolita! But she still had the post office. And, she was to go on vacation now to her home in Tamazunchale where she would be seeing Julio. He still had another year or two at school. No doubt, from now on Lola would be going home to see her mother more often.

Doña Dawn returned with the news that they had now laid sweet little Cousin Tina to rest. Also, they had found another place for Marcos to live right after I had returned a few weeks before. Don Julio was certainly glad to have her back after that extra long time. He never went to Mexico City himself, because he had a very severe heart attack there one time, and was never going to take a chance again in that high altitude.

Naturally, there were many sick people waiting for me, and it was good to feel more like working again. When my sick rounds took me to the edge of town, where the baby had been delivered by forceps, the mother would bring him out for me to see, saying, "Here's your baby." He certainly was a sweet one, chubby and smiling. Sometimes, I cuddled him awhile. And one day I took his picture tied to a little chair. By this time there were many others who were "my babies."

Doña Dawn was sad these days. Besides the sorrow of losing her niece, she was receiving discouraging letters from Marcos lately. He was not well and was going to the doctor and taking injections. Nor did he like his new boarding place. "He should have stayed with his aunt where he felt more at home," she complained. But in my opinion, he had stayed there too long, and I was fearful about what might be wrong.

Then, just when she and Don Julio were debating about whether she should go back to the City to see how sick Marcos really was, he surprised us all by coming home, saying that he had missed so many classes he didn't think he could pass the school year anyway. He was thin and pale, and everybody hoped that the country air would do him good. His mother consoled herself that he could continue his studies the next year. It was a good thing that she could not see into the future.

The doctor in town had prescribed daily injections which I applied, both of us looking forward to those visits.

During that time I taught him about Salvation by Grace through faith in Christ, which he accepted. He started to read the new Testament I gave him, and began to pray at night.

One day when we were talking about religion, I foolishly suggested that perhaps his father hadn't become an Evangelist because of his making and selling aguardiente. He laughingly said, "Oh, I don't think that has anything to do with it. He doesn't make much on it, he's just one of a company, you see."

Was I embarrassed when later I found that he had told

his Dad what I had said! "Oh, Marcos, why did you tell him, or rather, why did I talk so much? Maybe he won't like me so well any more."

"Oh, don't worry about that, my little one; he just smiled and said to tell you not to worry; that's not why. And some day he will explain it all to you."

"Yes, he told me that when I first met him."

"It's something to do with an accident he had," he replied, "but Dad can explain it better than I."

Little did we think that the occasion would present itself at a sad time for all of us.

One day I arrived at the back of their house and saw they had visitors. I didn't want to barge in, but I did want to see Don Julio about something. So, I waited there in the patio in the shade of the banana and palm trees. Nearby stood Don Julio's fine steed, an Arabian Palomino. He wasn't even tied, and when I got bored waiting, the thought came that he might like a drink of water down at the creek, so I mounted him.

We were just slowly disappearing out of sight when Don Julio came to the door. What a scene! He yelled, "Somebody stop that girl! Get that horse!"

Marcos came running and caught the bridal, turning us around toward Don Julio, who was still shouting, red in the face.

"You don't have to lead him back, Marcos; we're doing all right."

"Yes, I know, but Dad doesn't."

When we reached Don Julio, Marcos tried to sooth him saying, "Now Dad, watch your blood pressure. Everything is under control. Take it easy."

"All right, all right! But that horse could have killed her if he had wanted to."

"Well, you see, he didn't, Dad. Perhaps the horse likes her, too," he drawled.

When his friend Ricardo from San Martin heard that Marcos wasn't well, he came to be with him. It seemed to bother Doña Dawn, but to humor her son and to see him laugh and sing, she took Ricardo in as one of the family. Now there was music in the big house on the plaza. One of the popular songs was "Ven, Mi Corazon Te Llama" (Come, my Heart is Calling Thee).

We had heard this song a lot in Mexico City, and it was one of those they played in Xochimilco. Ricardo and Marcos sang it beautifully together.

Even the little girls in the Casa Hogar, Children's Home, at the Mission in Tamazunchale were singing it.

Another song very popular in Mexico at the time was "Let Me Call You Sweetheart." Everybody asked me to sing it in English. And sometimes I used my Hawaiian guitar in doing so. Also the lovely Strauss Waltzes, and other classic and semi-classic music could be heard everywhere one went. Some of us long for the good old days as music is concerned.

"All Saints Day" came again, but this year Doña Dawn didn't have as much enthusiasm for the preparations as she had the year before.

Unfortunately, I told the boys how we celebrated Halloween in the States with parties, masquerading, ghosts in white shrouds and pumpkin heads. We made pumpkin faces and put candles in them. Ricardo and Marcos thought it all to be a great idea. That night, when it became dark, they put sheets around themselves, carried the lighted pumpkins on their heads and went up and down the streets, moaning and wailing like the dead, really frightening a lot of people.

114

The next day, Marcos was too sick to get out of bed. His grandmother said that God was punishing him for making fun of things that were sacred. And I knew it was all my fault, although it hadn't been my intention that they would act out what I had told them.

To myself, I had to admit that the wailing and moaning in the cool night air hadn't been good for his lungs. His Mother and Dad didn't say anything, but I knew that they were thinking the same thing and I surely felt chagrined. Even Marcos, who was always able to be cheerful, seemed sobered and apprehensive when I went to give him his injection that day.

That night he became much worse. The next morning they took him to San Felipe to a new young doctor who had been recommended highly to Don Julio. Doña Dawn and he stayed there with relatives, while Marcos was under treatment for pneumonia. Ricardo went along to help care for him nights, for there were times when he was delirious with fever. One morning, Don Julio sent me my horse from his pasture and took me along to see Marcos for he had been asking for me. We went by San Pedro for Don Julio to check on the day's work. Then, we took the river road to San Felipe.

On the way, he said, "If money can save my boy, it won't be lacking. I would sell everything I have to save his life."

"Yes, and then it would still be up to God," I replied. "But He can do miracles."

"You think I don't know that? I believe in Him, too," he reproved me somewhat gruffly. "But we all know God says, 'Help yourself and I'll help you.' "

"It doesn't seem to me that San Felipe would be the place for him to be cured," I ventured.

"Yes, I've been thinking that myself. We may have made a mistake. I'm going to see about that today."

The crisis seemed to be past, but Marcos was very weak. We counted those precious hours. Then, in the afternoon, when I asked Don Julio what time we were going back, his reply was that he was staying. He hadn't been able to see the Doctor yet and had decided to stay overnight. And they wanted me to stay, too.

"But I can't stay overnight," I protested. "I didn't tell the girls I would be away, and they will be worried. Also, there is a woman expecting to be delivered any time, very likely tonight."

I didn't want to mention it to them, but I was also concerned because I knew that our Chief, Don Domingo Grande, was probably plenty upset about my coming, and if I didn't get back that night, he would most likely send a commission to town early the next morning to complain to the Dales about it.

"Perhaps someone is here from Chapulhuacanito with whom she can return. I'll go to the plaza to see," Ricardo offered.

He came back saying, "No, I didn't find anyone, but someone suggested the mailman. He's getting ready to leave. Perhaps she could ride with him; he has to pass right by here."

I agreed to that and Don Julio said, "All right, if you insist on going, Mae, but I don't want to be responsible," he scowled. Then he offered me his revolver.

"But you will need it yourself tomorrow," I protested.

"No, I won't need it, for I am going at noon when there is practically no danger. Here, put it on," he insisted, as he took it off. Everyone laughed as they knew that his belt would not fit me. However, he draped it over my shoulder, with the heavy gun falling at the right place on my hip.

"Why, she looks like a "soldadera," girl soldier, of the Revolution in her felt hat and jacket," someone remarked.

"But, she wouldn't know how to work that thing. If she meets up with the real bandits, they'll take her and your revolver, too." another commented.

"Oh, yes, I do know," I protested. "Back home, I sometimes shot at tin cans on posts. And one winter, when I was visiting friends on our big river, the Susquehanna, we played a game with pistols. Someone would go upstream and throw tin cans on the broken ice floating down the current, then when the tin cans came by us, we would shoot at them."

"That really sounds like fun. It seems that they do know how to have fun up in the States after all," the boys agreed.

By this time, they had forgiven me for wanting to leave and everyone was in a better humor.

The mailman certainly wasn't pleased about the "extra baggage!" Don Julio had to persuade him by putting some money into his hand and assuring him that no one would hold him responsible if anything should happen.

He wouldn't talk, only grunted, as he prodded his mules along. But that was all right with me, as I wasn't in any mood to talk either, thinking about how sick Marcos was and wondering about his future.

Don Julio did not like what he saw and the conference with the young doctor was not encouraging. So,he made immediate plans to bring him on a stretcher to Chapulhuacanito to be taken to Tamazunchale and on to a specialist in Mexico City. They arrived home in Chapulhuacanito late that night and left at the break of dawn the next day, so I did not see them. Also, my patient was having her baby at the time, as I had expected.

It was a miserable day when they took him; winter rains had set in and the mud was terrible. They made a canopy over the canvas stretcher, wrapped him in blankets and tied him on, for the men would be slipping and stumbling over the hidden stones in the mud. There was a large group of men, cousins and friends who went along to help carry him.

The one who took charge was Fernando, an older half-brother. He was Don Julio's son by a previous marriage. He never came to their house when Doña Dawn was there, but today, no one was going to keep him from his brother's side.

Afterwards, Don Julio proudly told me how well Fernando managed, knowing just where to place the men, when to change relays, and where to choose the best of the rugged paths, always taking over the head of the stretcher at the most dangerous places.

Indeed, Fernando, who had a store in the plaza, was a fine, promising young man, who later became the first of Don Julio's sons to become Mayor of Tamazunchale.

Doña Dawn and Don Julio rode behind the sad procession in the rain that day. Everybody was hoping that Marcos would not have a set-back.

The next day I followed, anxious to find out how he had taken the trip. He had made the ordeal better than expected. And the doctor in town was preparing to take him and Doña Dawn to the City in his car the following day. They were taking him to a specialist in a sanitarium.

When I arrived at the hotel where they were staying, the patio and corridor were full of concerned friends and relatives, mostly men, who were accompanying the family at this critical time.

As I entered the room, Doña Dawn graciously greeted me, moving away to let me sit at Marcos side. "I knew you would come," he said smiling as he squeezed my hand.

I had come from church, and when he saw that I was carrying my Bible and hymm book, he asked if I had come to read and sing to him. "You may if you wish. What did they sing there tonight?" he asked.

I read a little, but singing was impossible with the lump in my throat.

"Was the trip in here very bad?" I asked.

"No, not really, everyone was trying to keep up my spirits."

"The fact is," his brother Luis remarked, "that he was the one keeping up our spirits."

"Yes, that's the way our Marcos is," his family all agreed.

"Write to me," he begged as we said goodbye. And of course I said that I would.

CHAPTER

16

The short heavy set man who stood panting at the door was the carpenter, Don Jose, from Huichilingo.

"Do you have an injection against snake bites, Señorita? My son-in-law, Lucas, was bitten out in a field by a very poisonous one."

"No, I don't. Sorry, but you see I have no refrigeration. You will have to get it in Salubridad, the government clinic, in Tamazunchale. You could take my horse," I suggested.

"No, I can run just as fast, so I will go now. But perhaps he will not last that long, and my daughter, has seven children by him," he sighed.

There was nothing else to do. I wrote a note to the doctor, we had prayer and he was on his way.

Would he be physically able to make such a long day's run, sixteen miles each way, I wondered. He did, but it was dusk before he returned.

About that time another runner from Huichilingo had come to say that Lucas was still alive. They were giving him all the native remedies they knew of, but he was in great pain, and frothing at the mouth. We hurried, but it was dark before we arrived.

He was now frothing blood, there was even an oozing

from his ears and eyes. After giving the first injection, that stopped, but he was delirious and very restless.

The brethren were all there in a circle around him, praying and quoting Scripture as they helped to keep watch throughout the night. Most of the time I sat by the little fire on the dirt floor. Several hours later, after the second injection, he quieted down and I curled up on a wooden bench against the bamboo wall to get a little nap before the break of day, remembering the Christmas night I spent there.

Lucas recovered, but it was a long, hard, slow struggle before he regained health. In the meantime there were to be setbacks.

Winter had come. December rains set in with mud, slimy, heavy, clay mud everywhere. Lola was going there to teach a reading class to the adults and to practice the Christmas program.

The brethren were finishing the mud walls of a new church, and Don Jose was finishing the doors and windows. They had ordered new hymn books from Mexico City and were planning to have the dedication of the chapel along with the Christmas program.

One day when Lola returned I asked "How is Don Lucas?"

"Well, he can stand up a little now. He says for you to send him more tonic."

"And the practice and your classes?" I asked.

"Oh, the children are very eager and excited, learning their parts well, but as for the classes, these men just don't want to learn Aztec. One of them said, 'We know Aztec, why doesn't Johnny Dale come to teach us English?' That made everybody laugh."

"There is something that is troubling me, though, Señorita," she added later. "There are rumors of persecution. They say there are threats to destroy the new church."

"Oh, I don't believe the people of Huichilingo would do that, Lola. They seem friendly enough."

"Yes, but they did put a lot of brethren in jail there when they first started to believe. That hasn't been so very long ago. The brethren are a bit apprehensive and may have some reason to be, the way things are these days. The real threat is that wicked Colonel from up in the mountains."

As Christmas drew near there was much sickness, and Lola came down with flu. So it was necessary for me to go in her place to finish up the practice of the program there.

We were having a bit of difficulty about the date, for Tamazunchale, the headquarters, had their program on Christmas Eve and our villages had to fit in, first one night and then another. So we finally set up a date which was for the coming week.

The young men joyfully started to gather tropical vines to decorate the rafters of the new building with pride and satisfaction. They had labored long and hard and had a right to be proud of their new, roomy chapel. A commission of young men went to town to get the new hymn books which had arrived, and to buy bits of tinsel, and red and green crepe paper to make streamers to intertwine with the vines on the rafters.

They brought news! "We cannot have our program tomorrow night. We must wait until the next night," they announced, "for Friholia is having theirs tomorrow. Can you come over to practice one more time?" they begged.

"Well, I suppose I could come tonight, but I sure am busy. However, it is moonlight just now, so perhaps I could come back early."

And so it was arranged. I went and consoled the people that it would be just as well to wait one more night. Since all things work together for good, it sure turned out that it was supposed to be that way, for our safety.

The next night the people had retired early, when all the dogs began to bark as one hundred and twenty armed men on horses rode into town shooting pistols and shouting, "Death to the Protestants, and to the Gringos* with their foreign religion."

What a surprise! When they rode up to the Church they found it dark, with nobody there to kill! They had been informed that this was the big night. In their anger, they tore up the Bibles and hymn books, making a bonfire with them. Then they broke the lamps, windows and new doors and tried to burn the building down. But new mud walls do not burn readily, and some of the little chapel was saved.

Next, they attacked the homes of the believers, but they had fled out into the cornfields and woods. A few had gone down to hide by the creek. All of them could get away but brother Lucas. Poor man, he couldn't walk very well, as yet. So they invaded his home, bound him with ropes and dragged him out to a cliff overlooking the creek at its deepest part. They threw him over the precipice into the water some forty feet below, expecting that they were now ridding their part of the world of at least one heretic.

But down there along the bank several brethren were hiding. When they heard the big splash, they jumped in and pulled brother Lucas out, wrapping him in their own blankets they carried him over the hills to me in Chapulhuacanito.

It was not yet dawn when the little party of refugees arrived, trembling with cold and excitement. Now poor brother

*See Glossary, pages 173-174

Lucas got pneumonia, and it looked as though his wife might yet become a widow, and his seven children orphans.

But God, who had so miraculously saved him up to now, helped us to see him through this also. After much care and prayer, he passed the crisis and lived.

The men who attacked that night were none other than those of the colonel of Tehuacan from the mountains of Hidalgo. Word came that they were still stamping around in the little village, eating and drinking all there was in that small place.

All the while they were threatening to come over to our town to finish us off, including me that foreign woman.

Señor Flores, now our new Mayor, said it would be best if I went to town until this blew over. For he reasoned, "We cannot give you any protection against a large group of so-called soldiers like them. All I could muster here would be seven or eight deputies. However, I have sent word to the leader that they should not come across the state line, for we stand for law and liberty here in San Luis Potosi and would immediately inform the government. That should cause them to think. But I cannot guarantee that it will, for they are bad ones, a law unto themselves."

I considered leaving but figured that if I left the brethren would feel deserted and I was caring for Don Lucas who was in very critical condition in a borrowed hut nearby, so I decided to stay. Most of our Indian neighbors said we should go to sleep in huts farther away from the church, where perhaps we would not be found. They did, and took my girls with them. However, I decided to stay alone in my own house. I knew if they came the commotion and the dogs would waken me, and I had a hiding place in the bushes in back of the outdoor toilet all picked out to run to. I packed a small bag of my most important possessions and placed them beside my cot, ready to carry them with me, thinking they might burn down the house. So after committing myself to the Good Shepherd I slept fitfully for I was very weary.

They did not dare to come, not that far, but they did come up to the state line just outside of town where two of our families lived.

In one hut lived Julian, a fine young Indian boy, about eighteen, and his widowed mother. And in the other, his married sister, her husband and their little children.

A group of these terrorists, about eight, attacked them that night, by the moonlight. They took out Julian's brother-in-law, put a rope around his neck and started to hang him on a tree. They also shot into Julian's little hut, killing a hen that sat on a nest in a corner. That young man got his deer rifle and laying on the floor started shooting buckshot at them from an opening in the bamboo wall. He hit several so they left, yelling as they carried off their wounded. And just in time for Julian to get out and cut the rope to save his brother-in-law.

The next day these villians left the vicinity for the mountains they came from.

Now there was a lot of comment and criticism among the leaders of the church about Julian. They said that as a Christian he should not have taken up arms, that one should not be afraid to die, and so on.

When Sunday morning came Julian was there for Sunday School. When I saw him, he was standing alone looking dejected and puzzled, while gangs of whispering boys and groups of silent men stood around.

"Oh, Julian," I called, "am I glad to see you alive! That was fine work you did! You are a real hero, another David.

You really ran those Phillistines off that time!"

The boys then gathered around him and afterwards the brethren came forward and invited him to move his family in with them, asking if he was not afraid of another attack.

"Oh, no, I'm not afraid. God will take care of us as He always has," he answered with a smile.

And indeed, He did take care of all of us, for the only casualty of the whole vicious assault was the dead hen at Julian's house.

CHAPTER

17

Ramon, Pastor Julio's cousin whom we had visited in Lagunilla, was grinning like a happy school boy these days, his face puckering up to one side, because of a big ugly scar received in a drunken fight before he had been converted.

The reason he was so happy was that he had finally arranged to move to our village with his family of four little ones and a nice-looking step-daughter. He had now been given a small piece of government land for his very own, on which to plant beans and corn. The brethren had helped to build a little stick house for him. He was also contented because here at this new place he was able to go back and forth to his fields in the hills in a measure of safety; living without fear of persecution for the first time since becoming a Christian.

Even when the threats of danger had come close to us at Christmas time, it hadn't bothered him at all, for he was used to it.

In the few months he had lived here, he was an inspiration to even the older Christians, acting like a new convert in his first wonder of it all. We often refer to it as a new Christian's "first love." And in Ramon's case he wasn't going to live long enough to lose it.

The government land had belonged to Don Julio, who never tired of telling how he had given up land to the agricultural program started by his friend and former revolutionary general, Ex-President Cardenas.

Like most old soldiers, Don Julio didn't like to talk in detail of those terrible days. But, he would often say that because he fought on the side of the Revolution, he had been able to save his part of the country from the fearful ransacking and horrors which most places and innocent people suffered. Then when the war was over, he gave his share of land to carry out the ideals of the victorious party; for he was at least somewhat sensitive to the plight of the poor in their almost hopeless struggle for existence.

"At one time, my family owned all the land between here and the river at San Pedro, but we have parceled it off to the poor, and most of them are not even grateful," he complained. "Sometimes when I ride out the road between their fields, they glare at me as if they hate me, never even saying 'Buenos dias.' I have Indian blood, too." he would admit, "but, I declare, I will never be able to understand them."

The Indians had a different version of it all. They felt that they had only been given back a small portion of what had been all theirs in the first place before the Spanish came. Down in their hearts were resentments of injustices and cruelty which had been handed down from one generation to another, until hate and distrust had become so much a part of them that it seemed they were born that way.

One day while talking over the situation of the two peoples with our student preacher, Pastor Julio, I asked him, "Don't you think Christians could become neutral, liking and seeing both sides?"

He replied, "No, I don't think one can be neutral; either you are on one side or the other."

Knowing him to be of both bloods, I asked him point-blank, "Which side are you on?"

Without hesitating, he replied, "On that of the Indian; my mother is an Indian, and ever since I was old enough to understand anything, I have seen how she has suffered from my father and his family. Besides, the Spanish always overrule in every instance, whether it is fair or not."

As for young Julio's family, the case was that his father was indeed the "Don Juan" type. Although his mother was a beautiful, stately woman, with the regal, graceful bearing of an Indian princess, her husband was never satisfied with her. One of his affairs had been with our beloved, Doña Linda, a widow who was enticed by him before she became a Christian. The pathetic little sick boy of hers who died was the son of Julio's father, who in due time left her for another. Any man who would desert women like Julio's mother and Doña Linda wouln't be worth much in my opinion, although he was a tall, quite impressive-looking person.

That Pastor Julio had a Christian sense of love and forgiveness was evident in that he was kind and affectionate to Doña Linda, always calling her "Tia" (Aunt) Linda. Also, that he preferred the Indian type could be seen in that he chose Lolita, who seemed in every way like a sweet Indian girl.

He sometimes visited with and had cordial relations with Don Julio and his sons, because he was educated enough to show respect and mingle with the Spanish-speaking. Nor did he ever cease to pray for his father and his people. Years later, he was to have the satisfaction of seeing his father reunited with his mother and their family, and of seeing his father converted before he died. And with maturity, he himself became more neutral and tolerant toward the Spanish, identifying with them.

Don Julio had been pleased when in the course of our becoming acquainted I had told him how I had first entered the country in 1939 with a letter of permission given by President Cardenas allowing several social workers to enter Mexico to work in the rural sections; because of his deep interest in helping the Indian. Also, I mentioned that my missionary friend, William Townsend, who had made the arrangements, was an admirer and close friend of the President. He was writing a biography of him in English, "Lazaro Cardenas, the Mexican Democrat." Perhaps that connection helped to make our bonds of friendship stronger. We had so much in common that even though we differed about some things, we never clashed seriously.

One day, soon after Chrismas, Don Julio asked me if we "Evangelicals" had a sanitarium where they could take Marcos. "He isn't getting along well at that government-run place. We will have to find a good private one if he is to get well," he said with concern.

"No, we don't have any, I'm sorry to say. There are a few good hospitals but no sanitariums."

"Well, then, he will have to go to a Catholic one, run by the nuns. His mother has had a good one recommended to her. Only, you know what that will mean. I would rather see him in one of your religion. That's why I wanted to talk to you first."

Several weeks later, lonesome Don Julio was sitting in their patio under the banana trees, husking corn for his horses. When I arrived, he called, "Come sit down," as he folded a letter and put it in his pocket, looking very serious.

"Did you have good news," I asked hopefully.

"Yes, Marcos and his mother like the new sanitarium. The food and attention are very good so she feels she will be able to come home soon, leaving him in good hands. That part is good, but there is a problem, Mae. I hate to tell you this, but she seems to think that you should not write to him any more, that your letters may excite him and retard his recovery. So, Doña Dawn wants me to ask you to please not write to him any more."

What a shock! I was without words, as he continued while we both kept on husking corn. "Another reason, probably the real reason, is because of the religion. His mother has been upset because it seems he is being converted. Before he left here, he was reading his Bible and praying at night. As for me, you know I am in accord with your religion and feel as though I am more a part of it than of the other church. But his mother doesn't want him to change. She's tolerant about your religion being all right for you, but doesn't think it is for us. It is strange about Marcos, for the same thing, more or less, has happened to him that happened to me when I first heard and accepted the Gospel years ago. Remember, I told you about my friend Don Martin and how I helped him in his evangelistic work?"

"Yes, I remember, and you said that perhaps some day you would tell me what happened."

"Well, now is the time. You see, I was convinced that what my friend preached was the truth, and I was all for everybody else hearing about it, so I went around helping him to organize these churches. Then, something terrible happened to me. One morning, when I got up and started to put on my pants, a scorpion that had gotten in them during the night bit me on my leg. I let those pants drop mighty fast, and my revolver, which was still in them, went off, shooting me in the leg. I almost lost the leg and almost died of gangrene. A Japanese doctor who had come to Tamazunchale, saved me and my leg, but I was sick a long time and my leg still bothers me."

Now I knew why Don Julio limped. But I still wanted to know what happened that was related to the situation with Marcos, so I waited for him to finish his story.

"My mother said it was God punishing me for changing my religion. Now she says the same thing about Marcos, history repeating itself. It is indeed strange and confusing. Perhaps some of us are not supposed to be Protestants."

"But everybody goes through a time of testing, Don Julio, even Jesus was tempted in the wilderness."

"Yes, but certainly God doesn't want us to disobey our parents, nor to make our women folks unhappy. We know that religion means so much more to a woman than it does to a man; so we should let them have their way, at least in that," he reasoned. "I'm sorry that I have to talk to you about all this, my girl, but that's the way it is. Now, will you promise me not to write to him any more?"

"Yes, I will promise, if you will promise me that you will tell him why I am not writing."

"Certainly, we will tell him. That's understood. I will see to it," he promised. And I knew he sincerely meant it, and would do his part.

So, I kept my promise and hoped that they would keep theirs.

CHAPTER

18

The winter rains came and the mud was bad. Ramon now helped me part-time with the horse and accompanied me on a few trips. One instance, which I remember, was on our way to town, when we saw a pitiful sight. A poor little donkey was stuck in the mud. He had sunk until there was no part of his legs showing at all, and was slowly dying there of hunger and thirst, baying desperately. One could see that it was impossible to rescue him, but I wondered why someone who carried a gun didn't shoot the poor animal and put him out of his misery. When I put my thoughts into words, Ramon was surprised.

"What, shoot him! Would you shoot a person who was dying?" he asked.

"No, but people are different; they have souls."

"How can you be sure an animal doesn't," he argued. "Perhaps he was a human being in a former life, and he may come back as one again; or at least his spirit might come back to haunt whoever would shoot him. Quien sabe?" Who knows.

I wondered if he was teasing or repeating things he heard in childhood stories; or was he serious? Who knows?

Ramon not only accompanied me, but also served as a guide to visitors who came and went.

At that time we had Evangelistic services in our church, with visiting preachers from Mexico City. Johnny Dale came with them, translating their messages into Aztec. At these times of special services, Don Julio, Sr. Flores and others of the town attended. The services were a success with twenty grownups added to the church. The couples had been living in common-law marriage so now they were being married and baptized at the same time. Some had babies hanging in their mothers' shawls, while the father held another, with little tots hanging onto their parents' skirts and pants.

One of the converts was a fine young man who later went to Rev. Dale's Bible School. His grey-haired mother was among those baptized. She had lost a son for the sake of the Gospel sometime before, when he was shot because of his stand for Christ.

At that time we had North American visitors, Tom and Iona Fountain, a new missionary couple with their little baby Sara, who was a novelty to our Indians. A baby so white that she hardly had any color at all, Andrea remarked.

I felt so sorry for these young recruits out in the country in the cold rain and mud. One morning they asked me if I thought it best for them to go that day as planned, or to stay and see if it would soon clear up. We had asked Don Julio to lend us horses, which had been brought for them. Truly, I didn't know what to advise them. Perhaps it would continue to rain and the road would become impassable for days, as it did when John Dale and Louise Whiteman were married and I could not get through the mud to attend the wedding in Mexico City.

In the end the Fountains decided to go, with Ramon being their guide. It rained and was cold, and Ramon didn't have a rubber raincape so he got chilled to the bones, becoming very sick. He had all the symptoms of malaria, but didn't respond to that treatment. He suffered terribly, saying, "My bones hurt so, I would rather die and go to be with the Lord."

We put newspapers up to cover the cracks in their new stick hut, but even the wood fire on the floor didn't help much; it was so cold and damp. I put a hot water bottle at his feet, but he didn't want it, complaining that it would make the heat go to his head.

The visiting preachers went to pray with him, giving him communion. Indeed, everybody was praying for Ramon, but he died within a week. God, for reasons known only to Himself, saw best to take him to his eternal home.

My horse got rheumatism also and was hardly usable, so he was out in Don Julio's pasture; for he said that maybe some good warm sunshine would cure him. With no horse to ride, I went slipping around in mud, which threatened to pull off my boots as I went on my sick calls. I was getting very worn out and was down to 96 pounds.

Then, as warmer weather came, I got into a mess of chicken lice. Maybe I was allergic to them, for I got an itchy rash which didn't want to go away.

These were the things that were not romantic about Mexico. But when I felt like complaining, I would remember my brothers in their fox holes and trenches over there in Europe, and I knew that I was better off in the Lord's army.

My horse wasn't the only one sick. Don Julio's fine imported palomino came down with something, and they had to hunt far and wide for a veterinarian.

Now, Don Julio's high blood pressure got the best of him, and he had a cardiac attack. It was a good thing that Doña

Dawn and La Chata were home at the time. He and the horse both recovered. Also, the news from the City was that Marcos was doing very well.

Doña Dawn was still very nice and friendly, but she didn't share her letters with me any more. In fact, we never mentioned letter writing, nor did I venture to inquire if they had kept their promise to tell Marcos why I had stopped writing.

One of my visitors was my dear friend Edith Van Reed from Reading, Pennsylvania. She had come as a missionary to Mexico and was planning to study nursing at the Baptist Hospital in Puebla so that she would become qualified to practice in Mexico.

Edith was a pretty girl, very light skin with black eyes and hair. She was also very large, tall and heavy, especially from her hips down.

I went to Tamazunchale to meet her and to bring her out to the village. Before leaving for town, I asked Don Julio to please send me two horses for us to use, for my lame horse was still out in pasture.

Edith had no riding clothes, and not having much money, she decided to buy some material she could wrap around herself while in the saddle, then use it afterward to make a dress. She had picked a bright pink cotton cloth.

When Don Julio's very short hired man came with the horses, one was a big old war horse, a retired veteran counting out his days in Don Julio's pasture, and the other one was a little black pony. There was no doubt about which horse was for which one of us!

When Edith got up on that magnificent animal wrapped in that bright pink material and I came tagging along on the

138

little black pony, we resembled Don Quixote and his man Sancho. All the people we passed on the trail looked at us in amazement; then when they thought we were safely past, they doubled up with laughter.

Don Julio was very much impressed by the enormous girl. "What a magnificent woman," he declared admiringly, "such plump arms and well-rounded legs!" We wondered if he put it on a bit heavy to tease Doña Dawn and me, because we were so small and thin. He probably was sincere about it though, because afterwards he always referred to Edith as that "splendid looking woman."

Edith went along with me on my sick calls and helped to treat the patients in the clinic. She was inspired and thrilled by the great need and the work. "This is what I want to do," she declared. "I am going to come back and help you when I graduate, Mae. You need help, so wait for me until I come." However, it was not to be that way.

One of the other things I remember about Edith's visit was that it was apple time in Mexico. They had little yellow and green apples in the market from up on the cooler plateau part of the country. We peeled and ate apples in every way they can be prepared, until she said she didn't dare look another apple in the face.

Another thing which was new to her was the way we had to boil our food. Not having a refrigerator, we had to boil all our leftovers, morning, noon and night. And since we were unable to get meat except on market day, we boiled and boiled it in order to eat meat for several days. When she left, she said in her drawling witty way, "I never had such a boiling good time."

Edith's ministry in Mexico was to be very short. Soon after she graduated from the hospital, she went to help a missionary family in a tropical village. There Edith contracted malaria which brought on complications which were fatal. She went back to Puebla and died in the hospital where she had trained, much to the surprise and sorrow of her friends.

CHAPTER

19

One day, Señor Flores, our mayor, asked me to go see a man who had been in a fight. They had passed new state laws so that he had to make out reports. The wounded had to be given first aid, then sent to town to the county health doctor, often times on stretchers. I had prepared several who were cut and shot for this difficult journey into town.

It was a very hot day and I had to climb a hill on the other side of town. The poor man had a scared, haunted look in his eyes as he held his stomach together. He had been slashed with a machete. It had cut through the flesh of the abdomen, laying his stomach open to view, but not cutting any of the vital organs. I taped him together and put him on sulfas, assuring him that he would live but needed to repent of his ways. His weeping mother agreed, and I hope he did also.

On the way back to town, I began to feel queer, sort of faint, then my knees started to shake. By the time I got back to Señor Flores at the Post Office, I was hardly able to walk. This seemed strange, and I didn't believe it to be caused by the wound and the blood, for I was used to that, and it had never affected me this way before.

Señor Flores asked me a few questions, then said, "I think you are coming down with an attack of malaria. We better get you home to bed quickly. They gave me an aspirin, and he called his oldest boy, telling him to carry my medical bag. Taking me by the arm, he helped me across the stepping stones; but when we got to the hill, I had to sit down at every upward curve, having to be pushed and pulled all the way up. When we got to my gate, he said, "Now you start on your quinine capsules right away and get to bed."

It wasn't dark yet, but I shut the door, got a jar of water, capsules and baking soda to put beside my bed and crawled in.

How we ever arrived there without being seen by the ever-watchful eyes of the neighbors is really a mystery. Lola had gone to a conference in town, taking Aurelia with her. So, I was alone, and since Andrea didn't see any light nor signs of life, she and everyone decided I must have been called out of town on an emergency. Nor did I think my condition serious enough to tell them.

That night was agony. I chilled with cold sweat, then burned up with more perspiration. All the while, my head felt too big and painful to raise off the pillow. I hung over the side of the cot to vomit, throwing up until there was nothing left but the desire to do so. Then, the dysentery took over, and by morning, I was too weak to get up and answer the door when someone called, making them all sure there was nobody home.

By afternoon, I felt able to boil a little water and put a new supply by my bed. Just when I thought about opening the house and calling someone, my knees started dancing again, and I had to go back to bed for another night of fever. The second night wasn't so bad. The medicine was taking effect, my body was cleaned out; so I slept somewhat.

The next morning, I opened the door and surprised everybody by saying that I had been there all the time. They were flabbergasted and chagrined to think that the Señorita was in bed sick with no one with her. That was unbelievable to them.

Doña Linda shed a few tears as she told me how she had come and then gone away the day before. "After all you do for the sick, to think that you, of all people, would be sick here alone." Now, they all brought me atole, thick corn starch, and teas, giving me all the attention that good neighbors would.

To everybody, the big thing was not the illness I suffered, but the fact that I had been alone. When I thought of how the house might have been full of well-meaning women, all giving their advice and remedies, and the patio full of men sitting, waiting to hear if I was going to live or die, I decided that perhaps I had been fortunate that nobody knew.

These days when if I so much as got my feet wet, I would get a chill and fever. It had been a long time since I had the pleasure of bathing with the girls in the creek.

Also, I now understood what my malaria patients meant by saying that the sun made them sick. They would say, "The sun gives me 'paludismo,' " malaria. Then I would explain to them that it couldn't possibly give it to us; the mosquitos did that. But now I learned that being in the direct hot sun would stir up the dormant germs and bring out the symptons of an attack. Also, extreme cold could do the same. Any sudden change of temperature or altitude would bring on a new attack, as I later learned in the many years chronic malaria has stayed with me.

CHAPTER

20

Now I had to go back to the hospital in Puebla for more treatment. This time, I became a bed patient. There was no touring of interesting places; fact is, I was contented to lie in a comfortable, flealess bed without anyone calling me to get up and treat them.

They found that I had low typhoid along with the ameobic dysentery. Also, that I had both kinds of malaria, the everyday attack and the every other day attack kind, which was unusual.

Edith was there studying at the time, and when I was better she and I attended church and took walks to the plaza together. Her humor and wit were good for me, and for everyone around her.

When the doctor gave his permission for me to leave, he advised, "I want to see you again in a few months. The way you are going, you won't live long. New attacks of malaria, along with what you already have, could be fatal, you know. It is my opinion that you should plan to go home on furlough soon."

"Will you put that in your medical report to Reverend Dale?" I asked.

"Yes, that is exactly what I intend to do," he replied.

Before I left home, I had asked permission to visit Marcos in the sanitarium. After conferring with Doña Dawn, Don Julio said, "Yes, of course, that's all right. La Chata is there and can take you to see him." How could they say otherwise, since I was a friend of the family and would do the same if it were any one of them.

Arriving in Mexico City from Puebla, I went to his aunt's house where a big surprise was waiting for me. When I arrived there and looked up at the balcony in front of their apartment, who was there leaning on the railing, but Marcos himself. I could hardly believe my eyes until he waved.

"Marcos, you are here!" I exclaimed. "I was going to the sanitarium to see you and now here you are!"

His smile was sweet as ever, but in his eyes there was something strange, a questioning hurt look. And it seemed there was a certain reserve or something different in his manner towards me.

After I had greeted the rest of the family, and made conversation with them the amount of time expected of me, Marcos and I went out on the balcony to talk by ourselves. He asked, looking very serious, "Would you really have come to see me, Mae?"

"Yes, of course, I asked permission of your father and he said I could, and I really intended to do so."

"It is difficult for me to believe that, after all these months, when you didn't even have the interest to write to me."

"Oh, but I did want to write. You mean they didn't tell you?"

"Tell me what?"

"That they made me promise to stop writing. And they promised to tell you why."

"So that's the way it is. I believe you Mae. Let's take a walk around the block. There's a small plaza on the next street with a little church where I go everyday."

The park was one of the many little plazitas of Mexico, a green refreshing oasis in the midst of skyscrapers, apartment houses and avenues of traffic in the big cosmopolitan city with its multitudes. Its secluded quiet atmosphere which included an old colonial mission type church, was an ideal setting for people to find peace and understanding.

When we had found a bench in the shade of the trees Marcos told me how sad and disillusioned he had been when no more letters arrived saying, "I know how germ conscious you are, Mae, so I decided that you did not want to receive my germ laden letters anymore."

Then as he told me about those long months in the hospital, he said, "In the Sanitarium there was a little nun who reminded me so much of you, she came in each morning and evening to say the rosary and pray for me, and God heard her prayers."

"I was praying too, even though I couldn't write."

"Yes, I know that now. God heard and answered all our prayers. In fact it took everybody's to pull me through, the shape I was in."

When we arrived at the house La Chata had news for us. She had just received a letter from home in which they said that it was not convenient for her mother to come for her so she was to go back home with me.

The next day I arrived with good news that my passport had been renewed. We were making plans to leave as soon as possible when in walked an elated Marcos announcing, "I'm going back home with you girls. The doctor has given me permission to go home and report back here in about six weeks."

"Home! Really! Home!" La Chata hugged him saying, "What a big surprise for our Papacito," dear father.

Yes, I thought, for Don Julio hadn't seen his son for almost a year now. And Marcos was indeed anxious to see him too.

"Do you have to take treatment along home?" La Chata asked.

"No, no medicines. I am completely well. The check-up is routine."

We took an overnight bus, taking turns to sit with each other. We were all too excited to sleep. It was a moonlit night, cactus stretched for miles as we crossed the desert, and passed the lights of the city of Pachuca on the opposite mountain side. The lights of a city are always so fascinating seen from a distance.

We talked about our plans. The immediate ones were that they would get horses in town and go right on home to surprise their parents. And I intended to stay over for a few days at the mission.

When I asked Marcos what he was going to do and if he intended to go on with his education, he said, "No, I have decided that my life is going to be in the country. My Dad needs me. He and Luis have been carrying a heavy load and I am going to stay to help him. I already have many ideas for improving the ranch."

"That will make your Father very happy, but what about your Mother? I fear she will be disappointed. She was so anxious for you to become a doctor."

"Well, she will have to adjust herself to it, after all, she has to concede about some things."

Yes, I thought, especially since they were conceding to her concerning religion. As for her attitude about me, I could very well understand, for I also felt that there were too many differences for Marcos and me to become serious. So I intended to be very tactful and careful, trying to keep her friendship, if possible, which fortunately, I did, so that we were friends as long as she lived.

CHAPTER

21

"So, it will be four years next month since you came here," Rev. Dale remarked. "To me, it seems like yesterday. How about you?"

"Sometimes it seems like a lifetime, one spent in a different out-of-the-way world, whose strange inhabitants are basically like the rest of the human race."

"According to the doctor's report and recommendation, you need to go on a furlough soon. Our new mission organization hasn't decided yet if the terms of service are to be four or five years. But in your case, and in case of illness, that is no problem. However, I hope you can hold out a while longer until the new girl, Eugenia Baron, learns her Spanish. I think she would be the one to fill in for you while you are gone. Perhaps we will send her to be with you over the Christmas vacation."

"Do not worry about the future," he added kindly. "We want you to come back here, but if the doctor feels you shouldn't, we can arrange for you to go to a higher climate."

"Could we arrange that I would be home for the Spring Missionary Convention in my church? They will need to know soon."

"By all means, you should be there for that."

So, in six months more or less, I should be going home.

That it would be with mixed emotions, there would be no doubt; but I knew that I would be ready to leave the mosquitos and fleas, chills and fevers at least. And it would be well to get away from my personal problems. By announcing my plans to go home, I could indirectly let the people in the village know that I had no intentions or hopes of getting married, and that would better public and personal relationships for me on both sides of the creek.

During the following months I saw very little of the Hervert family, all of us being very busy.

Sometimes La Chata came to have me help her bake birthday cakes in my little oven.

And one day Marcos stopped by on the way to town to ask if there was anything he could bring for me. Because of the looks he and his horse got from the neighbors, he did not try that again. And I was very glad not to be given much attention for I did not want the chief and his friends to go to the mission in town complaining about me as they did about almost everybody on the hill.

Then it happened! They went to town to complain, and at a time when least expected. It so happened that very early one morning, a worker of Don Julio's from San Pedro came, asking me to go see his wife who had a new baby and was very sick. Because she couldn't nurse the baby, it had cried all night. I had no horse, for mine was still out in pasture with rheumatism. So I hurried over to Don Julio's house with the man, hoping to use one of theirs. Marcos was about ready to leave for the ranch and they had an extra horse, which he saddled for me.

It was a beautiful morning for riding. We galloped along, leaving the Indian man some space behind. When we came to the fields of Pedro's brother, I saw him and Pedro peering out at us from the tall corn as though they were displeased. The fact was they left their milpa, field, that very moment to go and tell Don Domingo Grande that I was riding out in the country alone with Marcos, for they didn't connect the walking man with us. Don Domingo, the chief, sent them right on their way to Tamazunchale with the news.

Marcos left me at the sick woman's house and went on to take care of the workers in the fields.

The woman had a very bad breast abscess and needed the only antibiotic we had those days, the usual sulfadiazol. We also used salve and it opened and healed later on. But in the meantime, that very sweet little baby was starving, so I offered to take it home with me to give her a formula until the mother would be in condition to nurse it again. They agreed reluctantly, but when I was going to carry it in front of me on the horse, the father objected. He wanted to carry that precious bundle himself. He carried it on his back in a sling tied to a band held on his forehead.

When we passed the fields where we had seen the brethren, there was no one there, for they were well on their way to Tamazunchale. That really hurt, for I had done a lot for that family and it was all so uncalled for.

When Don Miguel came, saying I was to go with him to a village over toward San Martin to visit some brethren having trouble among themselves, I complained to him about how unjust it was as we rode along.

"Oh, don't let it bother you, Señorita," he consoled me. "Rev. Dale won't pay much attention to them, and they will get over it. They really do like you, only they are jealous of your friendships, even of your doctoring the people on the other side of the creek.

"You know," he added, "I've been in the same predicament you are in. When I was a rural school teacher, I had to try to keep friends with both sides and I found it wasn't easy. You know that my wife is strictly Spanish-speaking. That was an advantage with the Mestizos, Spanish speaking, but it was a drawback with the Indians."

Before we arrived at the village Don Miguel told me of the problem at hand, which he was supposed to help solve. He seemed concerned and embarrassed, for the fact was that he had been in it from the beginning. The story was that a new young Indian man who seemed to be well-off according to their standards, had come to live with the family of the leader in the congregation. He fell in love with a very young neighbor girl and wooed her Indian fashion, going to visit with the mother and taking her, a poor widow, corn and what not. In that way, he arranged the marriage with the mother and the girl's brothers.

The girl was only eleven, but she was tall for her age, and they had lied to the judge at San Martin, who married them, saying she was fifteen. Then the girl refused to live with him. The morning after the first night, her married brother found her prostrated at his doorstep, trembling with fear, crying so that they were moved to pity and took her in.

Then, the man went to the church elders and demanded her back, and her brother took her back to him, but the same thing happened again. So now the elders were threatening to put her brothers out of the church for sheltering her. One could see why there was trouble. The man, who seemed to be about thirty, looked like a bully, the caveman type. The girl, although a bit tall for her age, showed no sign of maturity. She was flat-chested and child-like with vacant innocent eyes.

154

After supper, the Indian Council began, all of the men sitting around in a circle. After the usual Bible reading and prayer and a long exhortation, they finally got down to the business at hand. The girl's brothers were reprimanded for taking the part of their sister, a married woman who should be obliged to live with her husband.

Then, that man, the husband, told a sad tale of how he had given her mother bushels of corn and much coffee and beans for the girl and had been badly cheated. He complained that she didn't want to have anything to do with him. And when she took his lunch to him in the field, she sat it down on a rock and ran away.

In the end, they did excommunicate the nice-looking young brothers, saying that they could not come to church until they delivered the girl. They were very apologetic and timidly said they were sorry, but they couldn't do anything with her. They had tried, however they couldn't let her die out in the sticks either. So they were willing to take the punishment.

We women were in the kitchen listening to everything. Sometimes, I stood in the doorway, with no voice nor vote but burning up about it all. I did express myself to the women there, and no doubt the men could hear. "Can't they see she is still a child? Why didn't he marry one of these nice bosomy young women who would appreciate a man like him?"

The girls giggled when I said that.

"Don't they know that they were at fault, lying to the judge about her age? If they would go back to him and tell the truth, he would annul that marriage mighty quick."

Later, when I said the same thing to Don Miguel, he replied, "Yes, and put us in jail or fine us heavily." He really had a problem.

Indianland was a man's world. At such times I was glad to be a North American woman. The women folks appreciated me, I'm sure, but I'm not so sure about some of the Indian men.

CHAPTER

22

One day when I returned from my sick calls Lola was almost in tears, as she told me the latest. The land next door had been sold to an Indian man named Tomas, and he was saying that we had to take our toilet off his property. "And that's not all, Señorita, he even says that he is going to have the brethren make you take down the fence, saying that it is over his line, and not only that fence but the one by the Church also."

"But, that's not his property."

"No, but he says the brethren will vote against us and take it down, so there can be a public path there again."

A public path, where our garden is by the bedroom window, was in itself a scare, but the prospect of losing the toilet again was too much! Even though I wasn't going to be around many more months myself, others would be coming to live there. And I wouldn't want to go up to that public "out-house" again even for a week. So, I took my troubles to Don Domingo Chico as usual.

He said, "Yes, it is true that Don Tomas bought the land and is saying those things. I don't understand how he got it, for the man who let you use the land said he would tell me when it would be up for sale."

"And what do you think about the fence? He even wants the Elders to take away the one by the Church."

"The one on his side, he may be able to make you move back a little, but as for the one by the Church, I just don't believe the Elders would do that. We voted for the fence to be put up, and I don't believe anyone will vote to take it down. Don't worry, I will talk to my uncle about this. Why not tell Rev. Dale? Perhaps he still wants to buy it for the Church. I don't believe that Don Tomas really intends to live here."

Poor Domingo Chico. I knew he would do his best. He had always done all he could for me, but he sometimes had clashes with his uncle when trying to defend people. The fact was that he was having boundary troubles, too. And, sad to say, he wasn't going to win.

Andrea's oldest brother took for himself a common-law wife. She was not of the Church, and we didn't know her, but we did hope that perhaps this would be a change for the better for him. He was no longer the leader of the gang of single boys, but he had not changed. Now he was building a house of bamboo and had infringed on Don Domingo Chico's property by quite a few feet. Don Domingo Chico naturally objected, especially since it took property from his front yard right by the public path.

That young man wouldn't listen to reason, and his uncle, Don Domingo Grande, didn't force him to change his building plans. It always seemed that he was the Chief's pet, for he always excused him and his brothers because they were orphans, sons of his brother who died young.

Now that he was married, Andrea's brother had to find wood for his wife. At home he always made his younger brothers do it. The easiest place for him to find it was in our passageway. When the girls wanted to make tortillas on our mud stove in the morning, they would find the woodpile gone. That provoked us, because now we had to keep it inside our tiny kitchen at night.

These days, Ramon's widow and her oldest boy of about 12 were bringing our wood, and she was doing our washing also. Aside from this, she worked together with her boys in the fields. Her almost grown daughter now did housework in town, which was their biggest financial help in their struggle to survive.

The brethren were told by Rev. Dale to try buying the property from Don Tomas and he would pay for it, saying that he hoped to send them a native Pastor as soon as possible and they would need the lot to build a house for his family. They were able to buy it and the problem was solved.

Also, I was pleased to know that when Don Tomas presented his request to the Elders about taking down the fence by the Church, no one voted for it, not even the Chief. I was so grateful that I forgave him for complaining about me, and for opposing my medical work; and felt that perhaps he liked me after all in spite of my independent and strange new ways. When I got to thinking about it, I realized that I hadn't been to call at their house lately and perhaps they had reason to be jealous, as Don Miguel told me they were. So, I decided to go visit them at dinner time the next day and eat hot tortillas, corn cakes, with them again.

The girl who was to take my place was not a nurse, so it was a good thing when Dr. Acosta, my friend in the Health Department in Tamazunchale, used his influence with the government to have a man sent to open a small clinic in our village. This was the center of our thickly populated area, about 25 miles in diameter. Señor Flores also worked on that project, knowing that I needed to have some of the load taken off my shoulders.

Perhaps because of my sickness and medication, I was on edge about many things these days. It bothered me no end to sit in church with people coughing all around and even on me, many with T.B. Sometimes I would feel their hot breath on the back of my neck. Also they would spit on the damp dirt floor, many times hitting my shoes.

Toward the last, I started to wear a shawl and left my shoes outside the door as I entered the house, changing to slippers upon entering.

And how I always dreaded the funerals with their feasts and the contaminated cups they passed around! At these times I would say to myself, I'll soon be away from all of this, or think that perhaps this would be the last time. There was no doubt that I was really ready for a furlough.

CHAPTER

23

Not all was unpleasant these last few months, there were also extra pleasant things, along with the usual daily blessings.

One evening, Doña Dawn insisted that I stay for supper. They had venison and knew I liked it very much, for my own brothers were good hunters. It was a happy family party, and we continued to be in the same mood when La Chata, Marcos, Luis and Alva, his girl friend, walked me home. It as nice to see that sweet young couple acting affectionate and natural like normal sweethearts should; not trying to hide their interest like the Indian young people did.

Moonbeams danced on the sparkling water of our lovely mountain stream as we jumped across the stepping stones, which had now become familiar to me.

One day La Chata and Marcos brought Ricardo to visit. He was passing through and wanted to say "Hello." I served cookies and lemonade. The boys were in a jovial, teasing mood. About four o'clock the mosquitos started to come out from their daily retirement under the furniture, beginning to hum their wierd funeral drone.

"Listen to those mosquitos," Marcos remarked. "They sound like an orchestra. No wonder you have malaria all the time, Mae."

"Yes, isn't it strange," said La Chata, "and with your screen doors and screens on the windows."

"And we do spray a lot, don't we, Lola?"

"I'll tell you what's wrong," Marcos explained. "It's because they get in and can't get out again. We never have mosquitos hoarded in our house, now do we? Dad says it's because we have lots of ventilation."

I had to admit that they never seemed to bother me there.

"Why mice and rats couldn't even find their way out of here," he insisted.

The truth of the matter was that those hated things had been scaring me lately, taking the joy out of living in my "casita," dear little house.

"Anyway, I hate screen doors," Marcos continued. "They always slow up a person. If I ever build a house for you, Mae, it won't have screen doors."

I had no reason to believe that he was seriously thinking of building me a house. And to think of living in the kind of houses that were in Chapulhuacanito was not an attractive thought, and without screen doors it was unthinkable. Somehow, a screen door gave me a sense of security.

How was I to see into the future and know that one day he would build the most beautiful, expensive, modern house in Tamazunchale. Nor could I visualize that years later, this fun-loving young man with sometimes laughing eyes would be sitting, all serious and business-like behind the spacious Mayor's desk of that same growing city.

Marcos was proving to be a big help to his Dad's business, always pushing for progressive changes. He had big plans for the near future, saying it would not be difficult to develop a river road that would take their products from San Pedro to town by truck. Doña Dawn and La Chata could help Don Julio to have a wholesale house in Tamazunchale, where they would buy products brought in by the country people on donkeys and mules. The Herverts could then transport these products to Tampico via their trucking company. All of which would come to pass in the near future. Doña Dawn was now to have her dream of moving to town realized.

La Chata was also showing initiative and helpfulness. She had started a small school in their big living room for little girls to learn reading and writing. It surely made me feel good when I heard that Andrea's little niece and others of our Indian girls, who would not go to the public school, were attending and enjoying La Chata's classes. Perhaps, after all, I had helped somewhat to bridge the gulf between the two peoples.

While sweet, chubby La Chata was maturing into a fine young lady, she was not yet interested in spiritual things. However, it was she who would later become the active Evangelical Christian of her family.

One day Marcos said, "Mae, you look so sad these days. I have news that I believe will really lift your spirits."

"What is it? Do tell me."

"Dad has sold out his part of the aguardiente factory. Mother has been wanting that for a long time, and she's very happy about it."

"So am I, Marcos. That's really good news. I'm so glad."

Then, there was the day when Don Julio handed me a newspaper from Tampico. Below the headlines was the picture of the notorious bandit, Florencio Lara, who had murdered Don Pedro, his brother. He had been killed by the

163

Army at last. Others of his gang had been killed or captured. So it was a time of great satisfaction and relief, especially for Don Julio's family, as Julito would be coming home to his mother and would now be able to settle down to his education. This he did and very successfully, for he later became a Superintendent of Schools in Mexico City.

CHAPTER

24

Now that my days with them were numbered, the girls were sad. Aurelia was planning to go back to her relatives in the State of Hidalgo, on the other side of Pachuca to the little town of Alumbres. Doña Linda's oldest son Nico was talking about their going back there also, for they had heard that there was less persecution now in their "tierra," land.

Lola was going to stay on to help the new girl get started. Then, she and Pastor Julio were to be married in June.

Andrea had a new novio, and who would it be but Don Segundo's youngest son, Flavio, her other boy friend's brother. She married him soon after I was gone. We heard that Don Segundo had married a young woman. He never had the courage to come back to visit this place.

Rev. Dale had arranged that Nico, Doña Linda's son, would take my baggage on his donkey, and I was taking my rheumatic horse to sell to a man in town who said he could cure stiff horses.

Tomorrow I would be leaving early, and all day people had been coming to say goodbye. Dear Doña Linda and Ramon's widow with tears in their eyes told me how much they would miss me. Everybody asked when I was coming back or said, "Come back soon." Yes, I would be coming back at least to visit, for I had left things there, but not likely to stay, for I felt in my heart that this chapter of my life was coming to a close.

That evening I was having supper with the Herverts. It was the last time I was to watch Doña Dawn polish the lamps and the last time we would listen together for the beating of horses' hooves, and stand at the door to wave to the men as they came riding across the cobblestones toward us.

Marcos offered to take me across the square to say good-bye to his grandmother who was waiting for me under the roof of her rustic porch. "Write to me," she begged, "for I may not be here when you return." She looked so aged as she leaned on her cane that I wondered about that myself. Marcos offered to write for her which he did. I filled my letters to her with many verses from the Bible to give her faith and assurance for the future.

However, I did not need to worry about not seeing her again, for that remarkable lady lived to be within days of one hundred years old.

When we crossed the square again evening had come, and noisy birds were nestling in the spreading branches in the huge tree in the middle of the square. And welcoming lamp light was shining from the open door of the Hervert house.

At the table they all expressed their hopes that the war would soon be over and that I would see my brothers again while home in Pennsylvania, and fortunately we did meet again while I was there.

Don Julio said, "Take good treatment, get well soon and come back because we need you here."

When supper was over, Marcos and I sat on the door-step of the patio together. There were corn shucks nearby with their dry leaves rustling in the breeze, while the horses munched on their corn in the stalls.

The soft music of the radio made a nice background, mingled with the low voices of conversation inside where the family sat near the table in the lamplight. Outside, moonlight was shining on the shimmering leaves of the banana and palm trees.

Neither of us talked for a while. Then, as he studied my hand deep in thought, Marcos said, "You really don't intend to come back to stay with us, little one, do you? I have a feeling that this life is not for you — that it is not your destiny."

Now, as I stood on the ferry again, contemplating the swift current, so symbolic of swiftly rushing time and its changes, I hoped that I was a bit wiser and more mature than I had been a few years before.

This river, the hills and life beyond were no longer strange and mysterious. They had become a part of me.

There would be more to life — other places to live — other needy people to help — and above all a Message to give that makes trials and suffering worthwhile.

But, a bit of my heart would always be there "In the Heart of Mexico."

Epilogue

During the years since I left my first mission field in the tropics, which was in the early forties, most of the main characters of this book and I have kept somewhat in touch.

Lilia La Chata is married to a fine Christian man in Tamazunchale. She is the one of her family who has become an active Evangelical Christian. They have sent their children to Christian schools in the States. We visit occasionally as we travel north and south on our Pan-American Highways.

She took care of her mother and father, Doña Dawn and Don Julio, in their old age. Because of her Christian concern she brought both of them to a full trust in Christ and assurance of salvation before they died.

All of Don Julio's sons became mayors consecutively in growing Tamazunchale. They have always been helpful to the churches and missions of that area.

Pastor Julio and Lola Cuenca have been more closely connected with me. The two little boys I adopted are relatives of theirs; so the Cuenca boys became Royer boys and he is Tio Julio to them. Their stories are told in *Jewels of Mexico* and *More Jewels of Mexico*. At present Rev. Julio Cuenca is dean of a Bible school near Tamazunchale, which is sponsored by Bob Jones University. At this writing one of their sons is studying at that University in South Carolina.

The church and house on the hill in Chapulhuacanito now have tin roofs instead of the picturesque thatched roofs. There is a bumpy dirt road to the village, and a shaky bus runs the sixteen miles to it twice a day from Tamazunchale. Most of the forest has been cut down to pasture cattle, and a big cement bridge has taken the place of the wooden ferry that crossed the river.

The advancement of progress has brought many changes with the years. The medical needs of this and many areas of Mexico are now taken care of by The Government Program, which sends their newly graduated University medical students out to give a year of service to their country before starting private practice.

Mae Royer, 1941

1981, forty years later, on last visit to the village.

Glossary

Spanish vowels:
a — always as in ah
e — always as in our article a
i — always as in me,
    never our i
o — always as in no
u — always as in food

Spanish consonants:
h — is always silent
j — is like our English h
    (as in Jose, Ho-say)
ll — becomes y in
    Mexican Spanish
y — is like our e

In Spanish, que forms k and qui forms key.
In Aztec, hu forms w as in Huastecan, wuas-taken.

An a or an o at the end of a noun indicates its gender.
    masculine — tio — uncle   feminine — tia — aunt
An ito at the end of a noun makes it small or a term of endearment.
    casa — house, casito — little house or dear little house.

Definition of words and names used in this book:
    aquardiente — (water that bites teeth) sugar cane rum
    chato or chata — snubnose
    chico or chica — small or lesser, Don Domingo Chico
    chiquito or chiquita — little one or dear little one

173

curandero — (one who cures) witch doctor

Don and Doña — Mr. and Mrs., used in less formal way than Señor and Señora (Señorita — unmarried woman)

Evangelicos — name commonly used for Protestants

grande — big or great, Don Domingo Grande

Gringo — nickname of disrespect for people of the United States (Norte Americano, name of respect for them)

mestizos — people of mixed Indian and Spanish blood

plaza — park-like town square

Sinarquist — fanatical Fascist group that was active in World War II, also called Cristeros

Information

Orders for *In the Heart of Mexico* can be sent to F. K. Klopp Printing, P.O. Box 242, Lititz, PA 17543, U.S.A., or as advertised.

Information and book may be obtained by writing to the author at the above address, or at Apartado Postal 59, Montemorelos, N.L. 67500 Mexico.

Proceeds from this book will be used to support the Home, and for the education of needy children.